MW01292988

girls with grace...

grace at a glance

Christmas 2019

Kelley —
May you walk with grace
and may God always illumine
your way. Keep shining brightly!

XO

Gracemarie Serafina

Illustrated by Amanda Almich

Gracemarie Serafina

PAGE PUBLISHING, INC.
New York, NY

First originally published by Page Publishing, Inc. 2019

ISBN 978-1-64628-350-7 (Paperback)
ISBN 978-1-64462-698-6 (Hardcover)
ISBN 978-1-64462-697-9 (Digital)

Printed in the United States of America

To one of my dearest friends, Kathleen Carver. She is the epitome of a "Girl with Grace." She shines her authentic self always and is resilient even in the face of adversity.
You are my muse, I adore you! Merci.

Acknowledgment

THIS BOOK WOULDN'T HAVE COME to be if not for Debralynn Findon who had me teach a class of hers called "Image," a class for actors and models. It was there while teaching this class that I felt inspired to take it in further and make it my own. Debralynn has been in my corner for many years. Her belief in my talent as an actor and an inspirer of grace, empowerment, and manners is invaluable and graciously appreciated.

It is with gratitude to my marme and papa who I was blessed to have had as teachers, mentors, and encouragers. They gave me many opportunities to explore different interests and to use my imagination. Thank you for being living examples of integrity, truths, manners, and values, for it is these qualities that you showed that guide me and shape me. You taught me to see the beauty and goodness in all people and things. Mostly, thank you for giving me a foundation based on God and to know that with Him, all things are possible and that I am loved.

My sister Mary has always been my biggest fan. No matter what I have attempted in life, she is my champion rooting me on. And when I feel I have fallen short, it is she who shines a light on what good has come about. She is the most loving, kindest, gracious person I know.

To the rest of my siblings, Thomas, Patrick, Marc, Timothy, Lucia, Gemma, Christopher, and Bridget, you are all my favorites but for different reasons. The common thread is your goodness and kindness. You may have all thought me a bit out there, but you allowed me to flourish. Thank you for I know we all love each other and will always be there for one another.

To my Chi Omega sorority sisters who at a time in life when we go off to college and find ourselves alone and sometimes frightened became my new family. Your friendship gave me the courage to find my way and my purpose. To this day, I remember those times with deepest love and fondness.

Much love and appreciation to my Ellouise Theatre actors, Sandra Cruze, Sarah Hunter, Marianne Davis Rago, Betty Kane, Todd Worden, Jacquie Sullivan, Reynard Deegan, Sammantha Gregory, Tim Clifton, and Brian Aston with whom I have had the privilege to act with. You are treasured gifts to me. Your talents lift me up and make me feel valued and loved. You are my joy.

To my acting coach Steve Eastin whose constant belief and kindness in me gave me a playground to play and explore. You created a safe environment for me to discover my strengths and hone my craft, knowing I had nothing to fear and all to gain. You illumined in me the truths of living in the moment, to be a good listener, and that in my stillness grows beauty. I carry those truths in my everyday life. Merci.

Huge thanks to Tim Clifton who painstakingly guided me on how to put my manuscript on the computer. It is because of his tutorage that I am a bit savvier on the computer. He did it with a smile, making it fun, and never a sign of impatience.

Thank you, Todd Worden, my roommate, who has been there for me through the joys and sorrows of this my adventure walk. He reminds me to be grateful for every experience I have for this is what builds character. We are family, and I am blessed to know a man who is not afraid to come from their heart.

My love and gratitude to Peggy Miller who gave me a tool belt to use when fear or anxiety sets in. In those times, I just reach in, grab a tool, and breathe to walk forward. She taught me to be gentler and compassionate to myself and that I am enough. Her knowledge and beauty cascade down on me, when looking at her, I now can see my beauty and strengths.

There aren't enough words to express my deep appreciation for my publishers at Page Publishing. To Elliot and Kamie Butler, whose guidance, encouragement, faith, and willingness to stay the course and bring forth my vision so to illuminate grace to a world in need of manners. To the rest of my team whose names I do not know but equally of value to me, the editors and page layout of my book, thank you. You were always willing to meet me with my vision.

My deepest appreciation is for those who impacted my life and didn't even know it. They did it through their movies. Bette Davis showed me I could be strong. Audrey Hepburn showed me elegance, grace, style, and vulnerability. Jimmy Stewart taught me to have conviction and to be gentle and down to earth. Cary Grant showed me how to be charming and to have a sense of humor. Those two men have qualities I want in a husband. I always say, "I want a Jimmy Stewart and Cary Grant wrapped up in one."

Lastly, but most importantly, to my best friend, Jesus, who I talk with every day, sometimes even scream. I imagine in those times He laughs. He loves and believes in me completely. He plants seeds along my path and then lovingly guides me to be open to see them to fruition. I am grateful for all the wonderful people He has placed in my life who have passed on wisdom and have shown me how to live each day with gratitude, to be of service, and to shine brightly God's light through me so to spill onto all who cross my path. From the bottom of my heart, thank you!

Contents

Foreword

THIS BOOK IS A "PAY it forward." It is a 101 to social graces and empowerment of thyself. It is a great gift to anyone graduating eighth grade, high school, or college; celebrating a sweet sixteen or any birthday; Christmas; or just an anytime gift! You can always refer back to it when you need to remember how to set a table or when you might need a bit of encouragement or to be inspired to bring your best self forward. The beauty of it is that you can add on to it. It is meant to whet your interest in social graces and etiquette. My wish for all who read this finds that it adds value to your life in a small but important way. Because having social graces is important and will bring more success into your life.

Allow this book to motivate you to become all that God created you to be which is more magnificent that you can imagine!

Thank you for allowing me to share with you, and in so doing, I am inspired to illuminate my best self!

Who Is a Girl with Grace?

We are a sisterhood of Social Graces. A girl with grace is all women from birth to a hundred plus. We are young ladies who treat ourselves and others with respect and dignity! Always willing to listen and hear others points of view. We find the common ground to work in the highest good of all and do so with civility. We are always on the path to betterment. We do this by being brave courageous warriors who dare to be our unique self, shining our light brightly to guide our path and the paths of others who may need encouragement. We remember with gratitude where we came from and give praise to always know we are connected to something bigger than ourselves. I know that to be God, but you may call it the Universe or God, for it is the Source of all Good. Knowing this and claiming this, we realize we are based in love. We achieve our dreams and desires because they are divinely guided and in the highest good of all concerned.

Girls with Grace are intelligent and well-read. We have manners and value the art of etiquette. Knowing it is becoming a dying art, we are girls whose goal is to keep it alive by being examples.

We are girls who like being girls for we know our strengths and cherish our uniqueness. We are girls who admire and support all girls whether they come from different cultures, ethnicities, religions, or political views. We are not indoctrinated because we use our brains to discover truths based in facts. We lead gently but hold strongly to our convictions. We are empowering and inspiring with a can-do attitude.

We are daughters, sisters, wives, mothers, and friends. We not only excel in scholastics but also athletically. We have an innate knowledge that we are more than capable of achieving whatever career we choose. Be it artist, teacher, solider, caregiver, doctor, homemaker, mechanic, or president of a company or the United States!

We are Girls with Grace! We are unique, confident, graceful, and powerful in our own self!

Gorgeous, Intelligent, Respectful, Leaders! GIRL!

SELF-IMAGE

First impressions only take 15 TO 30 SECONDS! It is obviously about how we look, so look groomed! Be clean and neat, and dress appropriately!

Firm handshake
Eye contact
Smile

Be You. Be genuine.
Like yourself, accept you and own your power.
Value who you are and shine your light!

In the book *Shambhala: The Sacred Path of the Warrior*, this is how it describes the meaning of dignity and respect. It is my opinion that we must have these qualities in ourselves first so that we can treat others in the same manner.

Dignity: The degree of worth. The quality of being worthy of esteem or honor. Proper pride and self-respect.

Respect: To feel or show consideration, avoid intruding upon or interfering with others privacy. To be held in honor or esteem. Regard yourself and others courteously and kindly.

Sophistication

SOPHISTICATION IS THE ABILITY TO genuinely like you. To be able to be in any situation and act with grace and ease. You attain this ability by observing people, reading and through the art of conversation. It means gathering as much knowledge on as many topics as possible.

Be Someone Special

Remember it is more important to be useful than popular. Stand strong in your beliefs with conviction. Volunteer. Be the example. By being of service, you can not only help others see their worth but you also see yours. You can be the change.

First Impressions

Remember first impressions take only about fifteen to thirty seconds. So shine your authentic self.

Introduce yourself clearly and with pride.

Shake hands when introduced to someone, strong and firm. Men only shake hands with a woman when she offers her hand.

Have eye contact.

Smile. A smile that comes from the heart and is sincere is what creates a connection.

Work with your voice. Tone and inflection is what creates part of your charm.

Listen with your eyes and ears. Be gracious even if what they are saying does not interest you.

A successful person is interested in what other people have to say, the places and experiences that they have encountered on their journey.

When you see others' hardships and challenges, you realize your life is not that bad. Have a heart of gratitude.

Only share your problems with a person you trust that can uplift you and empower you forward.

When you share a story, remember that brevity is what will keep it witty.

Nothing is more off-putting then a person who thinks that they are a fountain of information.

Be proud of the things you have accomplished.

Bring your best qualities forward.

Have enthusiasm.

Learn to say you're sorry, to apologize.

Do not speak unkindly of yourself.

Do not speak unkindly of your family or from where you come.

Be able to laugh at yourself.

Compliment people's accomplishments.

Practice listening.

Keep sharpening your brain in all areas, even ones that are not all that interesting to you.

Knowledge is powerful when used correctly and factually.

Be well versed about what is happening in the world.

Talk about things that interest your listeners as well as yourself.

The only bad manners are those that are mean and meant to be unkind.

Shine your unique self forth; do not hide your fabulous self because others are threatened by your light. Shine brighter, and it will help them to know they too can shine theirs.

Pay it forward.

Be of gratitude always.

Believe in Yourself

THE WORD *CONFIDENCE* MEANS A sincere belief and trust in something or someone. When applied to the individual it means reliance on one's own God-given gifts and abilities to care for yourself. When we develop faith in ourselves, and a belief in our abilities to succeed, we can then free our minds of fear, frustration, and failure. Confidence is the peace of mind that brings success and joy where doubt and stinking thinking existed before. As we become more confident and self-reliant, we are able to be of better service to others.

Cultivation of the mind is necessary as food to the body.
—Cicero

Believe in yourself.
Learn to depend on yourself.
Think positively.
Create the best impression of yourself.
Let the way you carry yourself express assurance in yourself.
Develop genuine appreciation of your positive qualities.
Be self-determined.
Do not underestimate yourself.
Know your worth. Know the art of negotiation on a job interview. When offered a salary, if it is not what you feel you are worth; don't get emotional, just breathe. It is okay to say, "No, thank you."
Be original and be sincere.
Do not be afraid to shine your light brightly.
Remember, you are what you think; so use your words carefully and wisely.

Remember to use your edit button before you speak.

You cannot hold a torch to light another's path without brightening your own!

You need:

- A good attitude

- Ability to present reasons and augments with good sense and sound judgment

- Respect toward yourself and others

- Pride that is free from ego and vanity

- Faith in your ability to succeed

- Ambition to constantly strive for self-improvement

- To be genuinely interested in other people

- Be able to apologize and not to hold a grudge

Quickly list the things you like about yourself!

_____

_____

_____

_____

_____

List the things you know you need to improve to make you more successful!

_____

_____

_____

_____

_____

What do I succeed in/what comes easily to me that I am good at!

_____

_____

_____

_____

_____

Who did God create me to be? Who am I?

_____

_____

_____

_____

_____

Stress Management Tips

STRESS IS FEAR OF CHANGE, whether it is good or bad.

Eat healthy, colorful foods; organic is best. Remember to take your vitamins.

Do something every day that brings you joy.

Take care of your body by getting outside, or going to the gym. Just get up and walk; move!

Make a list each day of the things that you need or want to do. Put the one you fear first so that you get it done and will not obsess about it all day.

Know the difference between major and minor challenges.

Simplify.

When you feel yourself in a panic or experiencing anxiety, stop and take a few deep breaths. Say a few affirmations… "All is well with me, I am good enough."

Surround yourself with those who are empowering and where peace resides.

Live in the moment. It is really all we have.

If you come across a serious challenge, take a break for a short time, then return to the challenge and tackle it.

The art of compromise leads to successful relationships. Ask yourself, "In the big picture is this really important?"

When work becomes overwhelming, lists always help put things in perspective and assist in getting the task at hand done.

Perfection is overrated! Just do your best!

It is good to be competitive but not to be a bully.

Get enough sleep.

It is okay to say no. Do not do anything you do not want to or feel force to do. Learn to set boundaries.

Be realistic in your expectations of yourself and others.

Keep the child in you alive. Daydream, play, and keep your imagination thriving.

Do what makes you happy, and then success will follow.

Finish what you start. Give it your all!

Let your unique self shine forth.

Take responsibility for your mistakes but not the mistakes of others.

A strong person—a successful person—is one who can ask for help!

Know and value who you are. When you surround yourself with the right people your life will be happier. You are worthy! Have fun!

21 Empowering Steps for Girls with Grace

1. Give people more than they expect and do it cheerfully.

2. Marry a man you love to talk to. As you get older, their conversational skills will be as important as any other.

3. Don't believe all you hear; spend all you have, or sleep all you want.

4. When you say "I love you," mean it.

5. When you say "I'm sorry," look the person in the eye.

6. Be engaged at least six months before you get married.

7. Believe in love at first sight.

8. Never laugh at anyone's dreams. People who don't have dreams don't have much.

9. Love deeply and passionately. You might get hurt, but it's the only way to live life completely.

10. In disagreements, fight fairly. No name-calling.

11. Don't judge people by their relatives.

12. Talk slowly, but think quickly.

13. When someone asks you a question you don't want to answer, smile and ask, "Why do you want to know?"

14. Remember that great love and great achievements involve great risk.

15. Say "bless you" when you hear someone sneeze.

16. When you lose, don't lose the lesson.

17. Remember the three R's: respect for self, respect for others, and responsibility for all your actions.

18. Don't let a little dispute injure a great friendship.

19. When you realize you've made a mistake, take immediate steps to correct it.

20. Smile when picking up the phone. The caller will hear it in your voice

21. Spend some time alone.

(Author unknown)

Beauty Tips

THIS IS WONDERFUL, ESPECIALLY COMING from Audrey Hepburn, who was a carrier for the Belgian Underground Anti-Nazi Movement in World War II when she was only a teenager. She was a very brave and good woman; whose advice is sterling.

"Beauty Tips" by Audrey Hepburn

1. For attractive lips, speak words of kindness.

2. For lovely eyes, seek out the good in people.

3. For a slim figure, share your food with the hungry.

4. For beautiful hair, let a child run his or her fingers through it once a day.

5. For poise, walk with the knowledge you'll never walk alone.

6. People, even more than things, have to be restored, renewed, revived, reclaimed, and redeemed. Never throw out anybody. Remember, if you ever need a helping hand, you'll find one at the end of your arm. As you grow older, you will discover that you have two hands, one for helping yourself, the other for helping others.

7. The beauty of a woman is not in the clothes she wears, the figure that she carries, or the way she combs her hair. The beauty of a woman is seen in her eyes, because that is the doorway to her heart, the place where love resides. True beauty in a woman is reflected in her soul. It is the caring that she lovingly gives, the passion that she shows.

8. And the beauty of a woman only grows with passing years.

grooming

GROOMING

Body Hygiene

IT DOES NOT TAKE A lot of money to keep ourselves clean. It is important to bathe or shower every day or at least every other day. If you work out, then shower after. Use a body wash or soap with washcloth or shower sponge. This helps to exfoliate the skin.

After showering or bathing moisturize your body with body lotion. This will hydrate the skin and keep it soft and youthful.

Remember to use an SPF lotion if you are going to be in the sun!

Manicures and pedicures can be done once a month. There are plenty of places that do a wonderful job and cost anywhere from ten to fifteen dollars for a manicure and the same for a pedicure. They also offer a price for both if done together, which will be a deal!

Taking care of ourselves helps us to feel better about ourselves and shows that we care about and like ourselves. It also makes a good impression to others, especially when going on a job interview or interviews of any sort!

Flawless Skin

With all the first impressions you make every day, it's worth spending five to ten minutes to look your best!

Three basic steps for you to do morning and night that will have your skin looking vibrant and youthful.

Cleansing

Cleansers remove dirt and impurities. Never go to bed without cleansing. Lukewarm water is the best. After a thorough rinse, finish with a cool splash to refresh and revitalize skin. Being too rough on your skin can cause strain on the delicate collagen and fibers below the surface and cause sagging and wrinkling. Be gentle when washing your face.

Toner

A toner refreshes and brings the skin to the appropriate pH level. It also removes dirt that the cleanser may not have gotten.

Moisturizer

Moisturizer restores your skin to its natural softness by compensating for a lack of natural moisture. It keeps the skin hydrated and soft. A SPF of at least 25 should be used during the day. Apply moisturizer to the face, neck, and chest.

I suggest a facial four times a year. An aesthetician will evaluate your skin. She then can refer a cleansing routine and products that best suit your skin type.

I like Verabella skincare line. You can call them directly and they will help you choose the best products for your skin type and have them mailed to you. If you're ever in LA, make an appointment with them. It is a quaint boutique salon. Vera and staff are excellent. You will feel like you've come home for the holidays.

When in the sun protect skin with **sunblock**! I suggest a 50 SPF.

CANCER IS NOT FUN AND IS SERIOUS!

Helpful Tips on Taking Care of Your Skin

Do not pick your pimples. If not done correctly is spreads the bacteria and causes pimples to spread and irritates your skin.

Go to an aesthetician or dermatologist!

If you wake up and throughout the day a pimple develops, do not touch. At night, you can put a dab of toothpaste or a zit zapper ointment on it. It will help to dry it out and heal more quickly.

Puffy eyes: make chamomile tea and then dip a cotton pad in the tea and put on the eyes for a few minutes. It is soothing and calming to the eyes and helps reduce puffiness. Sliced cucumbers on eyes help too!

There are products you can get at the drug store that you roll around the eyes that will reduce puffiness too.

Makeup Tips

You do not need to wear makeup every day. It is good to let the skin breathe from time to time. Make-up should only enhance your natural beauty. Remember, less is more. It is important to take make-up off at night! I know sometimes we are so tired; but just do it. If left on, it ages the skin!

Go get a make-up lesson! They will teach you how to apply make up for you. You can go to any department store and they will do it for free if you buy even one of their products. This is one of the ways you can decide on what line of product work best for you.

I like La Bella Donna minerals. It is referred by dermatologists. The products have a SPF in them and are from natural minerals which are terrific for the skin.

You can find La Bella Donna by going to **labelladonna.com**. It is my favorite. It gives great coverage.

On Lipstick and Perfume

Less is more! Do not let your lips or your perfume enter the room before you do!

When we take pride in our appearance we feel better about ourselves and bring our best self forward!

Grooming/Hair

Our hair is one of the things people see the most. Just like the rest of our body, it is important to be clean. You do not need to wash hair every day for that can take away the natural oils our hair needs. Every other day is just fine. If your hair looks oily or stringy then wash it! If by chance you can't then pull it back and put a nice smelling gel to help it stay neat and smell good.

Hair length and style is always your choice. However, there are great guidelines to length and style which have to do with the shape of your face and the texture of your hair. Pull out pictures that you like and then consult with your hair stylist.

When your hair is looking like it has split ends, it is time for at least a trim. This also helps hair to grow faster.

Use a nice shampoo and conditioner. Again this will be according to your hair texture. It does not have to be costly! Suave is a great brand with many shampoos and conditioners to choose from.

Taking Care of Our Teeth

Brush teeth at least twice a day. Brush your teeth when you wake up and before going to bed.

Use an electric toothbrush or a toothbrush that has soft bristles. Brushing teeth too hard can cause gum problems.

Floss teeth! Floss after meals. Get in the habit of flossing. Floss teeth at least once a day. I put floss in every purse I carry and leave one in the car.

Use mouthwash for extra protection and freshness. I will suggest *Act* mouthwash. *Biotene* mouthwash is good if you have dry mouth. Dry mouth is caused by bacteria and will create problems for your health.

Go to the dentist at least once a year. But I will stress going twice a year to get cleaning.

Our dental hygiene is very important to the rest of our health. A healthy mouth is a healthy body and happy smile!

Grooming Test

The following is a grooming test for you to give yourself. Be honest, or it will not teach you what you may need to learn. On each question, rate yourself from 4 to 0. If you always do what the question asks, give yourself a 4; if you do it sometimes, a 3; once in a while, a 2; rarely, a 1; and never, a 0. If the question solicits a yes-no response, give yourself a 4 for yes and a 0 for no.

Do you take a bath or a shower every day?

Do you moisturize after bathing?

Do you use perfume?

Do you use deodorant?

Do you shave or wax the hair from your armpits regularly?

Are your clothes free from perspiration marks?

Do you eat a healthy diet?

Do you get enough sleep?

Do you exercise at least three times a week?

Do you wear clean undergarments?

Do you avoid using pins to adjust your clothes?

Are you getting missing buttons or torn seams repaired before wearing?

Are your clothes wrinkle-free?

Are your clothes clean?

Do your keep your slip or bra strap from showing (unless it is part of the fashion)?

Do you keep a neat and organized closet and dresser?

Do you dress appropriately for the occasion?

Do you look in the mirror before leaving to make sure you are looking your best?

Do you shampoo your hair often enough to keep it clean?

Do you cleanse you face morning and night?

Do you use moisturizer on your face after washing morning and at night?

Do you avoid squeezing pimples or blackheads?

Do you avoid frowning and squinting?

Do you see your dentist at least once a year?

Do you brush your teeth after meals and in the morning and before bed?

Do you floss your teeth at least once a day?

Is your toothbrush in good condition with soft bristles?

Do you make sure your breath is smelling fresh and clean?

Do you moisturize your hands to keep them soft and smooth?

Do you manicure your nails and at an appropriate length?

Do you avoid biting your nails?

Do you give yourself or get a pedicure at least once a month?

Do you use nail polish? And remember to remove nail polish when it begins to chip?

Do you shave or wax the hair from your legs regularly?

Do you feel well-groomed?

After adding up your score, compare it to the following:

> 180–192: You are an example for others to follow
> 160–180: Well groomed
> 130–160: There are areas that could be improved
> 100–130: New personal hygiene habits are necessary
> Below 100: Not well groomed

Take notice of the areas you need to improve on. Then work on them until they become a habit. Good grooming takes time and energy, not money to accomplish. It helps you to feel good about yourself and to bring you best self forward.

Nutrition

Food nourishes us. It gives us energy to perform though our day.

It should be thought of as a friend, not an enemy!

Simply put—anything in moderation!

The basic food groups are: fats, carbohydrates and proteins. I will list below some of the healthy ones in each category.

Proteins

Meat	Poultry
Seafood	Eggs
Low-fat cottage cheese	Tofu

Carbohydrates

Baked potato	Squash
Sweet potato	Pumpkin
Yam	Steamed brown rice
Steamed wild rice	Quinoa (it is a grain also it is high in protein) Millet, buck-wheat, bulgur
Oatmeal	Barley
Beans, red, black, garbanzo, white, lima, etc.	Edamame. Lentils
Corn	Fat-free yogurt/ Greek yogurt
100% Whole grain breads, cereal, or pasta, pancakes, waffles.	

Vegetables

Broccoli	Eggplant
Asparagus	Lettuce (not ice berg, no nutrition)
Carrot/Celery/Cucumbers	Spinach / Kale / Collard Greens
Cauliflower	Tomato
Green beans	Peas
Peppers	Brussels sprouts

Vegetables Continued	
Mushrooms	Artichoke
Cabbage	Radishes
Zucchini	Jicama/Okra
Onion	Sprouts
Beets	

Fruits (Remember fruits are high in natural sugar, and sugar is a carbohydrate)	
Apples	Mangoes
Pears	Melons
Peaches	Bananas
Nectarines	Oranges
Berries	Grapefruit
Cherries	Tangerines
Papayas/Pineapple	Kiwi

Healthy Fats	
Olive oil/Extra Virgin Coconut Oil/Flaxseed Oil/Pumpkin Seed Oil	Butter/Peanut Butter/Almond Butter/Cashew Butter, etc.
Cheese	Cream
Mayonnaise	Sour Cream
Avocado	

Nuts	
Almonds	Pistachios
Cashews	Hazelnut
Walnuts	Pecans

Foods You Can Have as Much As You Like	
Garlic	Ginger
Spices	Herbs
Vinegar	Mustard
Lemon/lime juice	Hot Sauce/Tabasco
Flavor extracts (almond, peppermint, vanilla, anise, etc.)	
SALT sparingly. There is salt in almost everything. Taste before salting!	

Beverages	
Whole Milk	Coconut Milk
Almond Milk (Vanilla, Chocolate)	Rice Milk
Coconut Water	Tea/Coffee
Herbal Tea	Green Teas

Fresh-squeezed juices: (Remember they are high in sugar.) Really best to only squeeze one fruit and drink that. You wouldn't eat more than one in one sitting, so why would you drink more than one.

Alcoholic drinks: Beer, wine. Spirits in moderation, and as a treat. Always when you are of age to drink!

Water: Drink 8 to 10 glasses a day. Not only does it hydrate us, it helps to carry away what our body doesn't need. I think of it like this: water is to the body what oil is to a car!

Vitamins: When we eat natural foods with vibrant colors we get all the vitamins we need. However, taking vitamins is a good supplement. So talk to a nutritionist to gain the knowledge you need for your body.

My favorite supplement is **Zeal**. It is an all-in-one natural nutritional drink. A synergistic blend of whole food concentrates providing an excellent source of nutrients, antioxidants and vitamins. I love it because instead of having to swallow twenty or more pills, I get all the vitamins I need with one scoop in water or juice. Just shake and drink. It tastes good too! You can find more information on line at: **zealforlifeproducts.com**.

It is best to eat organic foods.

Eat meat that is grass-fed, no hormones, free of antibiotics and can roam free and are cage-free. Eat fish that is wild not farmed.

When eating fruits and vegetables, best to buy from a farmers' market and those that do not use chemical sprays. They are most delicious when eaten in season. That is when they taste the best.

How to Eat for Brain Power

Max Lugavere is an American health and science journalist, author, and filmmaker. His mother, at an early age, developed cognitive impairment which prompted him to delve into research on foods and lifestyles that can help keep at bay memory loss and Alzheimer's. Here are a few suggestions that when incorporated into your diet will have a profound effect on your body as well as your brain:

Eat colorful foods. Spinach, carrots, peppers, yams, cauliflower, zucchini, beets.

Eat "good fats." Olive oil; coconut oil; avocados; butter, even better, Ghee (clarified butter); cream cheese, ricotta cheese, hard cheeses (all full fat).

Eat nuts. Walnuts, hazelnuts, almonds, cashews.

Eggs, red meat, bacon, dark meat. All in moderation. My Papa who was a doctor said lamb is the highest in protein and easiest to digest.

Eat anchovies, sardines, mackerel, herring, salmon, whitefish, eel, carp and butterfish—all good fatty fish and good for us.

Better to eat gluten-free. Of course, if you don't have an intolerance to wheat or celiac disease you can eat breads and pasta. I do my best to at home be gluten-free.

Wonderful spices to incorporate are parsley, rosemary, thyme, turmeric, cinnamon, nutmeg, cayenne pepper, and ginger.

Lemon water in the morning jump starts our metabolism. Organic raw, unfiltered, unpasteurized apple cider vinegar promotes healthy skin, digestion, balances your pH levels, helps with joint pain as it has anti-inflammatory properties and lessens symptoms of diabetes and obesity. Studies also showed it can help regulate blood pressure and lower cholesterol. Take a shot in the morning by itself or add to your lemon water.

Sugar substitutes for baking, adding to drinks and adding to foods are: maple syrup, agave nectar, coconut sugar, honey, cranberries, raisins, dates, cinnamon, brown rice syrup, pureed banana, and molasses.

To learn more on eating this way you can read Max's book *Genius Foods* and go to **maxlugavere.com**. Another good source to learn about this way of eating is **The Keto Diet**.

An incredible and easy way to help improve memory is to take wild organic blueberries which are high in antioxidants. Antioxidants help fight the free radical that attacks your cellular structure as well as DNA. Blueberries also have benefits for the nervous system and for brain health. Research shows new evidence that blueberries can improve memory. In a study involving older adults (with an average age of seventy-six years), 12 weeks of drinking 2 to 2 1/2 cups of blueberry juice daily was enough to improve scores on two different tests of cognitive function including memory. The easiest way to add this to your daily diet is to take it in pill form or powder. I have done my own research and purchase from **traversebayfarms.com**. You can get either the Organic Wild Blueberry Whole Fruit Powder (1 3oz bag is a 94-day supply) or the Wild Blueberry Brain Support Capsules (60-day supply). On this site, you can learn how they turn the blueberries into a powder and pill form. There are also videos on health benefits of their products. Very informative and interesting.

Another great supplement to add to your daily diet is SuperBeets (go to **hummann.com** to buy). Beets are high in vitamin C, fiber, potassium and B vitamin folate. They help to lower blood pressure, boost stamina, fight inflammation, help ward off cancer, good for your bones, liver, and pancreas, and help purify your liver and blood.

Remember that by eating right and not skipping meals will help keep our metabolism going. Think of food to the body is like wood to a fire. When keeping a fire burning, you add wood slowly throughout the day and it maintains the flame. If you forget about the fire and it is almost out, and then you add a huge log on, it suffocates the flame and it will go out! The same is true with food. If we skip meals and only eat one big meal a day, it slows our metabolism.

It is important that we do not get a mindset of deprivation because it will then only make us want the not so healthy foods more. So every week indulge in dessert!

Eating right and exercising balances us. It is that simple! Bless your food, take your time when eating, and enjoy the experience!

Remember that when you are kind and loving to yourself, and embrace the unique beauty God created you to be, you then will be able to have a positive healthy body image. Life will be joyful and less challenging!

We are all different. Find what works best for you that is fun and easy.

Exercise

It is important in life to keep moving. It is important to get up every day and do something to promote the health of our bodies so that we stay fit and energized. Exercise is not only good for the body but also our minds. It reduces stress and promotes healing and a good night's sleep. So many people say, "I can't; it hurts." Of course it will hurt at first because you do not move! But just start out slowly and in no time you will be able to do more. Exercise oxygenates the body and that is what stimulates circulation and promotes health and vitality!

Find whatever activity that you enjoy and do it. If nothing else get out every day and do at least a half-hour brisk walk.

Exercise does not have to, nor should, take up too much of your time unless you are an athlete. Three times a week for an hour is fantastic. Change up what you do so you won't get bored. When we get bored we have a tendency to quit.

There are many ways to accomplish this without having to pay too much. Tennis, swimming, hiking, running, biking, and rollerblading are just a few ideas.

Yoga, Pilates and dance classes may cost a bit more, but if it is what you enjoy you will find the money to do them.

Get on a sports team you enjoy. Not only will that help with keeping your body fit, it will also teach you how to be a team player and work well with people.

Join a gym. (Weight training and all sorts of fun classes are available with gym membership)

There are plenty of DVDs to choose from to do at home. Beach Body is a site that promotes fitness. There are many different exercise programs to choose and they even tell you how you can get a support coach for free. They also give you eating plans to assist you for healthy eating.

Some of my favorites are **_Supreme 90_** by Tom Holland**, _21-day Fix_** by Autumn Calabrese and **_PiYo_** by Chalene Johnson. They all take about 45 minutes total, including warm up and cool down.

Another way to honor and care for your body is by getting in a routine with massages and acupuncture. I know that people look upon massages as a luxury, but as a massage therapist, I am here to say that massages are the key to a healthy mind, body, and spirit. Massages along with acupuncture alleviate stress, oxygenates, and helps in maintaining proper body alignment. When we incorporate these two practices in our health routine, they help in keeping us healthy. A good massage therapist and acupuncturist can also assist in healthy eating habits and vitamin and herbal supplements to help maintain healthy immune system.

Now go out there and have fun staying fit!

Weight Control Tips

1. See yourself at the weight that you want to be.

2. Never use food for a reward.

3. Eat things that you like so that you don't feel deprived.

4. Eat at least 3 meals a day or 6 small ones.

5. Learn to love water—drink 8 to 10 glasses of water a day.

6. Cut out on sugar as much as possible. Sugar turns to fat.

7. Wait 10 to 20 minutes before going for seconds. If it is in front of us, we just eat it.

8. Read labels and nutrition books. The first 5 ingredients are most important. Make sure you can pronounce them.

Suggested Reading: _Body for Life_ by Bill Phillips

Tips On Doing Laundry

Separate clothes in piles of:
Dark Colors. Wash them in temperature Cold/Cold
Bright Colors. Wash them in temperature Warm/Cold
White Colors. Wash them in temperature Hot/Cold

Look on the labels of your clothes to see how they are to be clean. They will tell you if they should be dry-cleaned, hand-washed, or machine-washed, and if they can be put in the dyer or need to air dry.

On your white clothes, use Clorox or Oxiclean to keep them from looking dingy! You do not have to use it every time you do your whites, but I suggest doing it every third time washing them. I remember the time my Marme came to visit my sister Gemma and I and looked down at our whites to be washed and said, "Girls, don't you Clorox!" We got the message.

Some of my favorite detergents are Gain, Tide, Myers Lemon Verbena. Purex is a great detergent and has a reasonable price.

Fabric softener can be used to make clothes softer and static-free. I find it easiest to use the fabric sheets for the dryer.

Wash your bedding (sheets and pillowcases) every week. Wash your comforter/duvet every month.

Personal Style

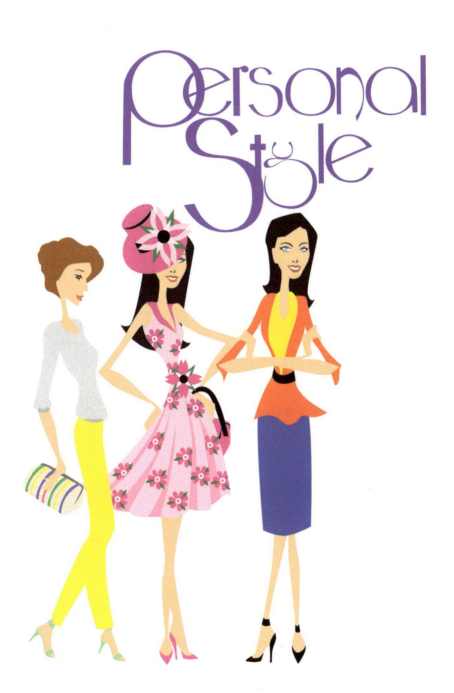

PERSONAL STYLE

PERSONAL STYLE IS JUST THAT—IT is personal! It should reflect your personality and shine your inner self forward. We must do our best to present our unique self with a sense of style and always with grace. Remember we are classy not trashy! Over the years, you will be influenced by society, trends, actors, models, teachers, and family to name a few. Your unique style will be shaped by those influences. You will hone your individual personal style over the years, and it will become clear to you when what you wear, how you speak, feels easy and comfortable, and positively you!

In the next few pages I will assist you on how you can achieve this and be able to bring your best self to light. Have fun! Remember there are no mistakes. Little mishaps in life, when we acknowledge them, reveal to us who we are, what we like and dislike. It is what helps us to grow into the best us we can be. So try on different looks and enjoy the process of discovering fabulous You!

Body Posture and Alignment

HEAD HELD UP. CHIN IS slightly down and not jutting out.
Hold shoulders back and down and relaxed.
Chest lifted.
Make sure there is a nice space between your last rib and your hip bone.
Stomach held in.
Pelvis slightly tilted forward.
Butt does not stick out in back and no big arch in your back.
Knees slightly bent and not locked.
Feet parallel and weight evenly centered between heel and toes.

Exercise strengthening your core which is your stomach and lower back. Sit ups and back exercises will help to do this. Make sure you do sit ups correctly; otherwise, it can make things worse. This will help with good posture. The core is where all your strength comes.

No slouching! People who are tall sometimes tend to slouch or round their shoulders, but just don't! Stand tall and proud!

How to Sit in a Chair

Sit up straight. Legs should be straight forward and knees together.

Or

Sit up straight. Sitting at an angle with knees together and ankles crossed.

It is best never to cross your legs as it throws hips out of alignment. But if you must, you can cross legs (knee over knee) but only when wearing pants.

Getting in and out of a Car

In: Face away from the seat, bend to sit with knees together onto seat. Shift weight back and lift legs into the car facing forward.

Out: Twist to face the door, keeping knees together; lift them up and out the door and stand up with the support of your hands to push you up.

Or

If you are on the driver side front or back: Twist to face the door, keeping knees together; lift them up and out the door. Cross right foot over left and stand up with the support of your hands to push you up.

If you are on the passenger side front or back: Twist to face the door, keeping knees together; lift them up and out the door. Cross left foot over right and stand up with the support of your hands to push you up.

This way you prevent exposing your undergarments when wearing a dress or skirt!

Personal Wardrobe

Your personal wardrobe should reflect your unique self. Listed below are some helpful suggestions to make it easier for you to achieve.

What is your height: tall, average, petite?
What is your bone structure: large, average, small?
What is your posture: erect or slouching?
What is your skin color: dark, olive, fair?
What is the shape of your face: oval, round, heart, square?
What is the color of your hair?
What is the color of your eyes?
Are your shoulders: broad, narrow, average?
Is your chest: small, average, large?
Is your waist: long, average, short?
Are your hips: broad, average, narrow?

What are your personality traits?

Are you conservative, sexy conservative, outgoing, shy, sophisticated, elegant, trendy, casual, a jetsetter, or a flower child? You may be a combination!

When you know your body and your personality, you can choose clothes that bring your best self forward.

Choose colors that best suit you. Get color draping done on yourself. It will tell you what shades are best for you!

When you own who you are then you can dress for success and feel good about yourself. Feeling good about yourself is attractive and draws people to you.

Always look your best! Whether you like it or not, people judge us on appearance.

Tips to achieve looking your best

Hair washed and neat.

Body bathed.

Make-up: not too much. It should only enhance your natural beauty.

Perfume: less is more.

Nails manicured. No chipping. Polish does not need to be worn all the time. Nails need to breath.

Clothes pressed and clean. Never sloppy! Even when going to the gym or grocery store. You never know who you may meet!

Shoes polished.

Not too many accessories.

Colors and How They Can Affect You Emotionally

COLORS NOT ONLY AFFECT HOW we look, but also how we feel and respond to various people, things and ideas. Much has been studied and written about color and its impact on our daily lives. The following is a list of colors and the energies that is connected to them.

Pink: love and beauty
Red: energy, action, confidence, and vitality
Blue: tranquility, youth, peace, truth, and spirituality
Grey: tranquility, security, and stability
Green: rebirth, life, nature, fertility, and well-being
Yellow: mental rebirth, wisdom, joy, and happiness
Orange: excitement
Black: (actually is not a color, it is the absence of color) Strength and stability
Brown: in touch with the earth (grounded)
White: taps the soul. Purity and cleanliness

It is interesting to see the meaning of colors. Look your favorite up and see what it means. Mine is Purple: royalty, magic, and mystery.

Insightful information on the meaning of colors, go to **crystal-cure.com/colormeaning**.

The Fourteen Point
Wardrobe/Accessory Check

THIS IS A TOOL TO assist in helping you look put together in a fun and fashionable way. My manager, Debralynn Findon, taught me this. I am sure this is something she learned while modeling. She taught that it is best to be between an 11 and 14 to have a finished look that is neither too busy nor too boring. In all things, bring your unique self forward.

Give yourself a point for each of the following: so if you have more than a 14, adjust your wardrobe.

Makeup
Hair
Hair accessory
Earrings rings
Bracelets necklace
Scarf
Nail polish
Shirt/Blouse
Pant/Skirt/shorts
Hat
Belt
Shoes
Toenail polish
Handbag
Blazer, jacket, coat or sweater
(Give an additional point for print and intensity of color)
(Don't count jewelry such as watch or wedding rings)

Dress for the Occasion

We have lost the dress code in society. People used to take pride in dressing for the occasion! We make excuses like: we don't have money or time or we say, "What's the big deal?" The big deal is that it shows respect for the event we are attending and respect for ourselves! When we dress a certain way our attitude changes. It is likened to an actor who when in costume becomes that person. Their mannerism changes, their walk, and even their appearance. Make it fun! Make it your own! Make the time! There is no excuse except, you don't care and don't want to! Why not be the inspiration for others! Plant the seed and watch it grow!

Tennis

It used to be everything was white. Now it is colorful. Wear a tennis skirt, dress, or shorts. A fun top that is tasteful. Tennis shoes which protect the court and your feet. Your sense of style but neat! Hair back.

Opera/Dance/Theatre

This is an opportunity to get dressed up! A lovely dress or it could even be full length or a pretty skirt with a sexy, nice top. If you don't like to wear dress, then a nice pantsuit or nice pants with a pretty blouse.

Wedding

Depends on the time! If it is an afternoon wedding, wear a simple dress or pretty skirt with a lovely top. If it is in the evening, wear a cocktail dress or pant suit. If the invitation says, "black tie," then an evening gown or a full-length skirt with a pretty blouse; but, very dressy. Always look well put together. No jeans! Classy not trashy!

Funeral

Dress with respect. Dark colors. A nice pants or skirt or dress.

Party/Music concert

Again, depends on where it is held. What the venue is. This is your time to make it you style and to be fun. Invitations give hints on how to dress.

Black tie

It is formal! No jeans. Men in tuxes and women in gowns. You are well put together; it is another chance to dress up.

Church

This is a place of reverence! So show it. It is best to wear a skirt or dress or nice pants. You should cover your shoulders. So if you wear a dress or shirt with straps; then just while in church put on a sweater or a wrap. If you wear jeans, wear a nice pair. Sometimes in beach communities, shorts are accepted; but once again, with dignity. No short shorts! Don't show your midriff. Have respect for the Lord and yourself.

There is a time and place to be sexy and flirty. Church is definitely not one of them!

Job Interview

This is when you put forth your best self!

No cell phone in hand or *on*.

No water or coffee in hand or brought in the interview room.

Not too much makeup or perfume.

Nails manicured. No outrageous colors; clear polish is best.

Dress clean and simple: no big bangles or big earrings. Wear a nice suit or dress. Clothes cleaned and pressed. Nothing short or too revealing!

Have your shoes shined, and wear an appropriate heel size. Remember you are going to an interview for a job; not clubbing with a friend!

Sit when offered a chair. Sit with good posture. Your hands crossed on lap and your legs crossed at the ankles. Back up and straight.

Breathe. Speak slowly, clearly and confidently! Listen! Do not give too much personal information.

Your resume should be done on good paper such as linen. Clean and kept in a portfolio to be handed out when asked.

Here is a link that will be helpful in composing your resume: **myperfectresume.com**. This site lets you choose a template to follow, then helps you build your resume, finalize it and then download.

Bring *your* best self forward and *smile* and have *fun*!

Dressing for the occasion is just another opportunity to use your sense of style appropriately, with fun and dignity!

Remember to wear a smile whenever possible.

It is important to be on time for any event! In life, it is all about planning!

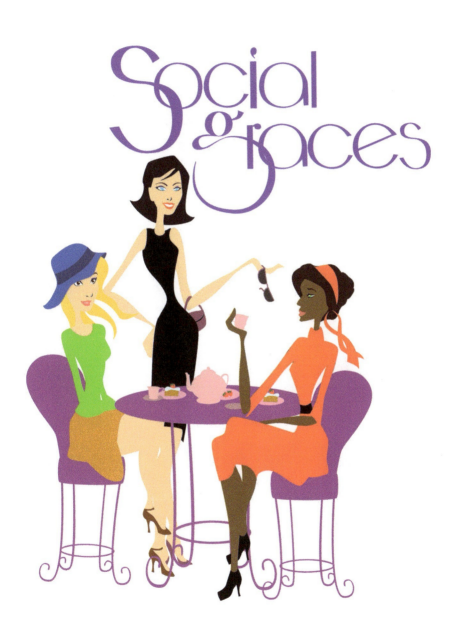

Social graces

SOCIAL GRACES

Etiquette History

To have proper etiquette and manners may seem like a thing of the past. It requires too much effort…why bother? But can you imagine what it would be like if we did not show common courtesies and kindness to others? We have, through the years, evolved in improving our standards of living and being gracious towards one another.

In early times, etiquette had two purposes having to do with status. First, it reminded people of what social class they were in and then how they were to behave within that status.

From about the fifth to the seventeenth century, etiquette dictated even on the level of bowing from a lower class person to a higher class person. It told of how long was proper for a man to court a woman before marrying her.

Even mourning had proper etiquette. Widows were expected to dress all in black with a black veil, known as the "widow's weeds," for a full year. This was done as recently as the mid-1800s. Today we still dress in black or dark colors when attending a funeral.

Mostly, rules of etiquette concerning marriage, mourning, and entertaining were for high society and the ruling class. It was especially important when addressing kings and queens. We still do this and also when addressing presidents, senators, congressmen, as well as the hierarchy in the Church.

Even peasants and workers had to know etiquette in order to get work and to properly respect their superiors. However, they did not have to follow as strictly the rules concerning marriage and mourning.

You can see how this worked by watching an episode of the BBC program, *Downton Abbey*.

Regardless of social status, we all should strive to act properly and with social graces. Etiquette today is not about power but more about putting others at ease with grace and respect.

Proper etiquette begins at home. It teaches us how to care for each other and for our belongings. Having the basic etiquette on table manners, communication, common courtesies, and corresponding will help us not only in our homes but in our work places and in public.

In the 1800s, people took great care of their homes. They worked hard but no matter how much money they made, they kept their homes painted and clean and inviting to welcome guests. As well as provided for the needs of their family. If you have the chance to visit some historical homes, notice how they kept their kitchen and dining areas.

George Washington at the age of sixteen wrote a handbook called *Rules of Civility* because he appreciated the value of manners and how they affect us. You can look it up on the internet and print out a copy. It is brilliant!

Table Setting

On the following pages, I will have a guideline on setting a proper table. It is used in restaurants, banquets, and homes. I often refer to it myself from time to time to make sure I have set it properly.

There will be a diagram below to assist you in setting your table; one diagram for Luncheon setting and one for Dinner setting. For the most part, forks are placed to the left of plate and the knives (cutting edge facing the plate) and spoons are on the right of the knife. When eating, use the flatware from the outside in, If the salad is served first, then the salad fork is on the outside.

Luncheon Place Setting

Place luncheon plate in center.

Bread and butter plate goes to the upper left of the luncheon plate.

If using a butter spreader, place horizontally across top of bread and butter plate

Set the place knife to the right of luncheon plate and the place fork to the left.

If you are serving soup as a main course, then place spoon to the immediate right of the knife. If the soup is the first course, then the spoon goes to the outside.

Place salad fork outside of the place fork unless salad is served after the entrée, in which case, place it inside.

Bring dessert spoon or fork to table at end of meal, if you wish.

Set water glass (the only glassware in a lunch place setting) at the tip of knife.

Wine glasses can be brought to the table.

Place folded napkin to the left of forks, or on luncheon plate. I sometimes put napkin in a ring and place on the luncheon plate.

Bring cups, saucers, and teaspoons to the table with dessert.

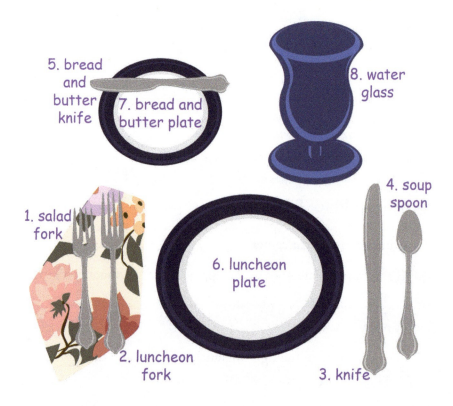

Dinner Place Setting

Place dinner plate in middle.

Set bread and butter plate (optional at an informal dinner) at the upper left of dinner plate.

Lay butter spreader horizontally across the top of plate.

Place knife to the right of dinner plate, cutting edge toward plate.

Set soup spoon to the right of knife.

Seafood fork goes to the right of soup spoon.

Place forks to the left of dinner plate in the order of use, from the outside in.

If a salad is served before the entrée place salad fork on the outside. If the salad is served after the entrée, then place salad fork to the right of place fork, next to plate.

Set water glass just above knife.

White wine glass goes to the right of water glass.

Red wine glass goes to the right of white wine glass.

Champagne flute goes to the right of red wine glass.

Place folded napkin to the left of fork or on plate.

Sometimes I like to put it in the wine glass. It makes a nice presentation.

Bring cups, saucers, and teaspoons to the table with dessert.

5. bread and butter knife

11. champagne flute

9. white wine goblet

8. water goblet

7. bread and butter plate

6. dinner plate

1. salad fork

10. red wine goblet

4. soup spoon

2. dinner fork

3. knife

Table Manners

1. Social graces are for everyone, not just for wealthy people or people with social status or higher education.

2. Do not take your seat at the table until hostess tells you to be seated.

3. The first person served is the lady guest of honor.

4. You wait until everyone is served before eating unless you are told to go ahead.

5. Place your napkin on your lap as soon as you sit down.

6. Use the fork that is furthest away from your plate when you start eating.

7. The difference between American and Continental style of eating is that with Continental style, you eat with your fork in your left hand. In American style, you switch your fork back to your right hand to eat.

8. When eating soup, tip the bowl away from you to get the last bit of it.

9. Soup served in a handled cup is drunk. If there is anything on top, eat first with a spoon.

10. Do not play with your food or smash it all together.

11. If food is too hot, take a drink of water.

12. You pass food to the right around the table.

13. Use a piece of bread to push food onto your fork. Never use your fingers.

14. Elbows are allowed on the table between courses, but it is best to never allow them on the table.

15. Chewing or talking with your mouth full is a No-No.

16. When you are finished dining, push your chair back into the table.

Helpful Tips When Dining

When eating spaghetti or long noodles: Using a fork rolled the noodles around fork. Do not slurp up your spaghetti!

When eating with chopsticks: Place the stick that will not move between the middle and ring finger at the base. The stick that moves is held between the tips of the pointer finger and thumb at the base. It takes some practice but be patient and have fun.

When you are finished eating, put the fork and knife together on the right side of the plate. If you are not finished eating, separate the knife and fork on either side of the plate.

If a drink has a garnish, eat it after you are finished the drink.

There are some foods you can eat with your hands. Listed below are a few:

Berries with stems on them
Asparagus as long as there is no sauce on them
Bacon
Artichokes
Corn on the cob
Chips, pretzels, etc.
French fries
Fried chicken

Hamburgers
Ribs
Hours d'oeuvre, canapés, and crudités

If you are not sure you can always look it up on the internet! If you are in the situation, then follow what the others are doing.

A general rule when using utensils is from the outside in.

How to Toast Properly

During a dinner, usually the host will give the first toast; however, a guest may do so as a way to thank the host for the event.

Toasts offered by others usually start when dessert is served.

Never bang on the glass to get the attention of people for a toast. The host should stand and then with voice gather people for the toast.

The person giving the toast will stand. If it is at dinner and is a small gathering, the person may sit.

If the person who is giving the toast stands, everyone else remains sitting including the person who is being toasted. The toaster may then ask everyone to stand to toast the person.

At the end of the toast, everyone takes a sip—*a **sip***, not the entire drink!

The person who is being toasted remains seated and does not take a drink to herself. The person being toasted just smiles and sits. She or he may acknowledge the toast with a thank you or then can offer a toast to the host or anyone else and will stand to do that.

When raising your glass to toast: if it is a general toast, look into the eyes of the person when clinking your glass.

When making a formal toast at say a wedding or business event: keep the toast short and relevant. To share a story, give praise, use humor, are all good things to include. It is okay to bring heart to your toast and be sentimental. **Just be authentic!**

Conversation

TO HAVE A GOOD CONVERSATION you need to be a good listener and be open and gracious.

Have eye contact. Don't interrupt. I know it is challenging because you have thought of something that adds to what they are saying, but take a breath and wait until they are finished to add on.

Be uplifting and stay away from complaining or gossiping about others.

Smile. Learn to take a compliment.

When a conversation is not that interesting to you, take a breath, stay with it, don't look around or be distracted as it will seem as if you don't want to be there. Engage by asking questions. You can learn much by listening. Also, it allows you to see what you may have in common. Then when there is a lull in the conversation, excuse yourself.

If discussing an important matter, repeat back what you heard them say and then say what you can do in helping the situation. Find common ground. Take ownership of your part in a situation and apologize if you need to. You can always agree to disagree. Always communicate with civility.

Be careful not to make it all about you.

Be gracious and interested in the other person and treat them with respect and dignity. Do not get too personal.

Do your best to stay away from politics, religion, and sex, unless it can be done with civility and respect.

Entertaining

<u>Guest</u>

1. Arrive promptly, or ten to fifteen minutes late.

2. When invited for dinner at 8 p.m., arrive a half-hour earlier.

3. Always RSVP to an invitation.

4. Say hello to everyone you know.

5. Do not interrupt a conversation because you are excited to see that person.

6. Never walk away from someone so they are left standing by themselves. Bring someone else in that you know has something in common with them and then exit.

7. The host or hostess is the person you say goodbye to last.

8. Send a thank you via email or through the mail. Sending the thank you through the mail is preferred.

Invitations

1. An informal invitation may be extended by telephone.

2. If invitation is by phone, then you may reply by phone.

3. When inviting over the phone be specific as to the day, time, and place of event.

4. It is not polite to ask, "What are you doing Friday evening?"

5. When sending an invitation for a casual gathering (a tea, luncheon, cocktail party, informal dinner, graduation party, housewarming party, pool party), it can be by mail, the phone or an evite. Send at least a few days to two weeks in advance of the event.

6. The invitation must include the day, the time, and the place of the event, as well as the attire.

7. You may reply to a written invitation through the mail, an email, or a phone call.

8. RSVP is the shortened version of the French phrase, "respondez, s'il vous plait," and means, "Please respond." And that means saying either "I am attending," or "I am not attending." It is rude not to do this as it is needed for the hostess to know how many will be attending so that she can properly prepare.

9. Formal invitations, for such events as a Wedding, Holiday dinner, Christmas party, Charity party, or a Debutante ball,

are written in the third person. And to be sent three to six weeks in advance.

10. For formal invitations, you must write out the date as well as the address and the person's name. Example:

    Sunday, June Second, Two Thousand Eighteen.
    Mr. Timothy (not Tim) Clarke
    222 West Elm Avenue
    Los Angeles, California.

11. When you accept an invitation to a wedding reception, a gift is a must. Even if you gave a present at a shower, you still must give a gift at the wedding.

12. You have one year to send a wedding gift. The bride has one year to send a thank you. It would much easier to do it right away if you have the time.

13. Gifts do not need to be sent in response to an announcement of marriage. However, it is your choice to send a gift, and then it would be mailed to the bride and groom after they are married.

14. The wedding gift, if mailed, should be sent to the bride even though you might be a close friend of the groom.

Two wonderful sites to help you with the dos and don'ts of writing invitations with examples are **emilypost.com** and **partyjoys.com**.

Public Speaking

DRESS IN YOUR UNIQUE STYLE. You must be true to your own personality.

Make a good first impression.

Do not show fear. Remember nervous energy and excitement are the same visceral reaction.

When speaking to someone, make eye contact.

Luck is when what you have been preparing for meets opportunity.

The knowledge of written and spoken language is a must.

Never condescend to an audience.

Go over a speech fifteen times if you need to. Do so out loud and in a monotone manner. This allows us to wrap our mouths around the words.

Practice in front of a mirror.

To show confidence and a knowing in your topic: Speak slowly and clearly. Wrap your mouth around your words, breathe, and know that it is okay to pause.

Articulate when speaking.

Read books or poetry out loud to practice.

Add energy and excitement, as well as various speeds to engage your audience.

To move up the ladder in your career you need to be able to clearly formulate and express your point of view.

We are always in the business of persuasion.

Have passion and energy when speaking. It will show you care.

Be aware of your audience. Are they responding negatively or positively to what you are saying? This way you can adjust to get them onboard with you.

You can move but do not pace, it will appear that you are nervous. Stand still with hands just below belly button palms up. This says, "I am here to give and to receive."

Use your voice. Project it out but do not yell. Remember to pause and breathe.

Dress appropriately, in sync with what your coworkers are wearing so that you look like you are all on the same team.

Don't smile constantly; come back to neutral. That is the place between the smile and the frown.

Do not dress sexy as it comes off as caring too much for the opposite sex. Remember we are classy not trashy.

If you are losing your audience, state the obvious it makes them aware and brings them back to the now.

Use your feelings sincerely to be able to connect with your audience.

Being prepared will assist with nervousness.

Use note cards with bullet points on it to keep you on track.

Practice saying tongue twisters to help with voice and articulation.

See and speak to the entire audience.

If you throat gets scratchy, drink water or swallow. If you feel self-conscious then share with the audience. "I feel like there is something in my throat." You will have them on your side.

Before you begin your speech, jump up and down, shake out your body. Take a few circle breaths in and out. It centers you.

Give yourself a pep talk: "I am good enough, I breathe, I listen and I illuminate the room to creativity, acceptance and kindness. I am well received and I receive graciously."

Your delivery should be natural as if you were speaking to a friend.

Know your topic inside and out so that you can go off on a personal story and then come back to your outlined point.

Suggested reading: *The Art of Public Speaking*

Correspondence

Manners may not be much in themselves but they are capable of adding a great deal to the value of everything else.

—Freya Stark

THIS IS WHY SENDING NOTES or cards via the mail is most important. Think, how do you feel when you receive a card in the mail? It makes you smile! To know someone took the time to sit and hand write a note or card makes you feel special.

Make a pact with yourself to acknowledge people's kind gestures with a card or note. When someone gives you a gift, or lends you something, or shows you an "out of the ordinary thoughtfulness or generosity," this is your opportunity to write a thank you. Sometimes it is nice to send a note just because you thought of the person and want to let them know you are grateful for their presence in your life.

When sending an email or writing a letter make sure you have the correct spelling of the person's name. Names are important to us. If you are unsure of how to spell the name, ask someone who knows them to give the correct spelling.

Pay attention when you are introduced to someone and the name that is given. If the person introduces themselves as Timothy, then that is what they want to be called. Americans tend to shorten names more so as a term of endearment; however, people always say their name as they want to be address. So, pay attention and honor them by calling them by that name. For instance, my name is Gracemarie and most people will say, "Oh, 'Grace,'" and I say "No. 'Gracemarie,' all one word; small 'm' connected to the small 'e.' Gracemarie.'"

Thank you cards should come from your heart and be written in your own person style. The note should include what you were given and how it will add to your life.

The inside of the card should address the name of the woman first and then the name of the man.

Example: *Dear Olivia and Max.*

Then on the envelope you address is *Mr. and Mrs. So and so.*

Examples of thank you cards:

> *Dear Thomas,*
>
> *Thank you for the lovely wallet. How did you know I needed one? Purple is my favorite color and every time I pull it out I will think of you fondly!*
> *I appreciate the thoughtfulness that went into my gift.*
>
> *My best,*
> *Emma*

> *Dear Mrs. Enterline and Mr. Enterline,*
>
> *The other day I was in a restaurant and someone commented on my posture and grace in which I held myself. They asked if I danced, to which I replied yes. In that moment I thought of you and how grateful I am to have had you as my first ballet teachers! Because of you I have a much deeper appreciation of the fine arts.*
> *Until next we meet, much joy and health!*
>
> *Warmest regards,*
> *Gracemarie*

Other reasons to send cards:

- Birthdays, weddings, engagement, birth announcements, and condolences. Or just because you thought of them and are grateful.

- Always be heartfelt and yourself!

The Difference between Text, Emails, and Letters!

We now correspond not only by letters; but also, via text and email. The lingo and writing is different in text and email. So, it is important that we not forget how to write a proper letter.

It is okay in a text message to not write out words or to use numbers to say what is needed; but it is not acceptable in letters or an email.

In emails, one does not necessarily have to address the person or sign your name; however, I still think we should. And an email still takes the form of a written letter.

Also in writing an email especially in business, be specific in the subject line. Make the message precise and to the point. If having a different thought or on another topic, best to write a new email with a new subject heading. This way when one needs to address a specific topic it will be easier to find. Less confusing!

Having the correct etiquette speaks volumes and sets us apart.

Correspondence in Business

Always send a thank you after an interview with a potential employer. Sometimes it could come down to you and someone else. The reason you may have gotten the job was, not only your qualifications, but also that you had manners. You wrote a note of thanks. When you go above and beyond it is noticed and appreciated.

Example note:

> *Dear _____,*
>
> > *It was a pleasure meeting with you today. I sincerely appreciate the opportunity to have shared my ideas. It would be an honor to be part of your team.*
> >
> > *Thank you for your consideration and time. I look forward to hearing from you soon.*
>
> *Sincerely,*
> *Kurt Taylor*

Letters of Resignation

As much as we may detest where we work, we must use grace in writing this letter. One never knows when we will meet up with this boss again and better to err on the side of kindness and civility.

It should be written in business letter format and directed to the immediate supervisor, with a copy to Human Resources. Include your intention to resign, why you are leaving, and the last day of work. It is a courtesy to give two weeks' notice.

Example letter:

> *Your address*
> *Today's date*
>
> *Employer's Address*
>
> *Dear (Name),*
>
> *Please accept my resignation effective as of (date of two weeks to the day).*

I am grateful for all I have learned and the experiences I have had during my five years of employment with (Company's name). I have decided to accept another opportunity which will enable me to further my career.

Sincerely,
(Your signature)
Your full name
Cc. Human Resource

How to Address an Envelope

In the upper left corner:

Your name
Your address
City and State and Zip code

In the middle of envelope:

The person to whom you are sending the card
The address
City and State and Zip code

Example:

April Finn   [Stamp here]
222 Apple Road
Roanoke, VA. 24003

Mr. James Holland
555 Endeavor Road
Charlottesville, VA. 22905

Phone Etiquette

It seems that we are in an era that has to be connected 24-7. I find this sad. I would like to encourage us all to get off our cell phones and connect in person. But since this is where we are, then let us be aware of phone manners.

Some Scenarios:

Proper phone etiquette is that we call between the hours of 9am and 9pm. This also means sending email and texts. The only exception to this is if the person you are calling grants you permission.

When calling someone at home ask for whom you are calling and identify yourself.

When answering, use a greeting and your name.

Examples:

When calling a residence
"Hello, the Lynch residence."
"Hello, is Michael home? This is David calling."

Or

"Good morning, the Lynch residence."
"Hello, Mrs. Lynch. Is Michael home? This is David."

Returning or calling a business

"Good afternoon. This is Emily returning Mr. Lewis' phone call. May I speak with him, please?"

Or

"Good morning, this is Emily calling in regards for the position available. May I please speak to Mr. Lewis?"

When making an appointment

"Hello, this is Alicia, and I would like to make an appointment to see the doctor. Is she available Tuesday, June 6 around 10 a.m.?"

Of course this seems formal, but the point is to remember our manners! Be who you are in your style but always with manners.

Cell Phones

Nowadays everyone has a cell phone. I realize that many have replaced the landline with the cell phone. However, unlike the landline, we often are in public when using our cell phone, therefore opening ourselves up to bad phone behavior. Cell phones are helpful when you are late for an appointment or your car breaks down. We use them more than ever in a manner that is disturbing the peace. We need to be conscious of our surroundings so that we don't walk into traffic or bump into others while talking on our cell. It is not worth hurting ourselves or others. Let us be the example as to when to use them. And remember to always turn off your phone when engaging with others.

When Never to Answer, Call Out, or Text

At the bank
At the grocery store
In church
On a date

With friends at coffee, lunch, dinner, etc.
Conducting business

If you are tempted, leave your phone in the car. If you are expecting an important call having to do with an emergency or business; then put your phone on vibrate. When you see it is the number you are expecting, either wait until your business is completed, or excuse yourself and go outside away from the public to conduct your call.

It is a nice touch to let the person you are with know that you are expecting an important call you have to take. When it comes in, you will excuse yourself for a moment. When you return to your friend, make sure your phone is off or on vibrate, and do not answer if it rings. It is rude to answer while in the presence of others.

Do Not Text!

In school
On a personal or business date
In the car

Texting should be quick bits of information!

Example: "Checking in, hope you are having a great day," *or* "I am running ten minutes late," *or* "I cannot talk right now, call you later."

Texting is not to be used to carry on a full in-depth conversation. Mostly because what you are conveying can be misunderstood.

We lived without cell phones for hundreds of years and got by just fine. People, even business, can wait an hour for you to respond.

When Leaving a Message on the Phone

State your name and number slowly and clearly and then the reason for your call. Close again by repeating your name and number slowly and clearly.

Business example:

"Hi, Katelyn. This is Judy at 818-322-8789 calling in regards to the receptionist job. I look forward to talking to you about this. Again, it is Judy at 818-322-8789. Have a lovely day."

If you are leaving a message for someone who is a friend you don't have to be so formal. However, it is still best to say your name and leave your number at the end always slowly and clearly. They may not have your number.

Example:

"Hi Marc, it's Sally, just calling to check in and see how you are doing. When you get a chance give me a call. My number is 212-555-1212. Have a nice day!"

Always listen to the message before returning the call. The person took the time to leave it, and it is frustrating for the person to repeat it because you didn't want to take the time to listen.

A phone call should be returned the day of if it is a business call. If it is a personal call you should return it that day if possible and no longer than 24/48 hours from when you received the call. If you know you aren't able to get back that day, this would be a time you could send a quick text saying that you received their call, that you are swamped and will get back to them in a day or so.

I always let friends know that if they need to hear back from me that day to please say that. Works like a charm.

Never hang up on a person! If the conversation is getting heated, let the person know that you need to table the conversation for now and will talk about it at another time. End it with a good bye and have a nice day.

Common Courtesy

I REMEMBER BEING TAUGHT...TREAT PEOPLE like you would like to be treated; when you point your finger there are three pointing back at you; don't judge a book by its cover; don't judge a person until you walk in their shoes; to be kind and respectful and to treat yourself and others with dignity. Yes, this can be challenging for us all, but let us do our best every day. When we do this we see the goodness, the God, in all of us. A collective energy of healing, encouragement, compassion and love goes out to the Universe and boomerangs back to us. In that moment, healing is at hand. The injustice, hurt, pain that we carried is lifted from us and we illuminate our path for the betterment of all. We forgive ourselves and others so that the chains that bound us are broken and we now move forward in that collective healing light to find peace and goodness. We can then work together for the common good of all. We do this by lifting each other up, instead or tearing each other apart. Joy and love and mercy are at hand!

Reminders of a Few Common Courtesies

Make sure to do your best to return a phone call or email within 24 to 48 hours, whether this is business or personal.

Hold a door open for someone

Give your seat to an elderly person, a pregnant woman, someone who is injured, or is carrying too much.

Respect your elders and respect yourself.

Respect those in uniform, the police, the fireman and those who serve in the military. Remember that every day they risk their lives to protect and defend our freedom and liberties. So next time you see one, go up to them and say, "Thank you for your service and for taking care of us." This small gesture of gratitude on your part will make their day. We all want to be appreciated.

Say, "I am sorry," or "I apologize."

Bathroom etiquette: Flush the toilet (use foot to flush when using public toilet). Wipe toilet seat down if necessary before using and after. Put lid down. Replace toilet paper if empty. Thoroughly wash your hands after going to the restroom. Keep the sink area neat. This is at home and in public restrooms.

Cover mouth when yawning.

Chew with your mouth closed and do not talk when mouth is full.

Do not apply makeup or lipstick in public. Go to the ladies' room.

When you sneeze or cough, do so into your elbow. This way you prevent germs from spreading.

When you burp, say, "Excuse me," or "Pardon me."

Take your sunglasses off when talking with someone. Eye contact is important and makes people feel important.

Remember to say thank you when someone lets you go in front of them in a line or especially when driving, a little wave is greatly appreciated.

We use our blinkers when driving.

Help when you can. Example, when someone asks for directions. When someone needs help crossing the street or help carrying groceries or packages.

When invited to a dinner or party, bring something such as flowers, bottle of wine, or dessert to show appreciation. And if they don't use it at the dinner or party, you don't get to take it back!

When staying in someone's home as a guest, keep your room and bathroom tidy. Bring a house gift and or take them out to dinner to show your appreciation. Send a thank you note through the mail!

When you borrow something and accidentally break it, say you are sorry and offer to replace it.

We ask to borrow things. And just because we received permission once does not give license to borrow again without asking.

It is okay to ask for help. You may be surprised to see all the assistance that comes your way.

Be on time! If running late, call to let the person know you are running late and be honest with how late you will be.

Put things back the way you found them.

Do not move other people's furniture to suit your needs when visiting them.

No feet on furniture unless it is a footstool or ottoman.

People who smoke you not only pollute your lungs, but also the air and other people's lungs. Most smokers throw their cigarette butts on the ground which is litter. Smoking is your choice, so be respectful to others as you indirectly are taking away their choice to not smoke by having to smell and inhale secondhand smoke. It is my opinion to just not smoke! Choose not to for your health. Smoking is not sexy; your clothes smell as well as your breath.

Do not litter! Remember: "The world is not a garbage can!"

When walking your dog, big or small, please pick up the poop.

When someone does something nice for you, "pay it forward."

When sharing on FB or other social media, do so with civility. Remember everyone has opinions and you can agree to disagree. Also, feelings are not facts; so, if in a discussion of politics, religion, history, etc. get the facts. Weigh both sides to make an informed and factual opinion.

When in a Business Meeting

Be on time!

No smartphones in meetings. Even if you are taking notes or looking up pertinent information having to do with the meeting, it comes across as bored, distracted, and disrespectful. So unless otherwise permitted by the person heading the meeting, no smartphones.

Volunteer! This is a great tool to help you when feeling down. It enables you to get out of yourself and help someone else feel better. In turn, it makes you feel good. Go to a nursing home or an assisted living and ask who doesn't get many visitors. Then go visit those people. Bring flowers or chocolates. Sit with them and ask them about their lives. What was it like where they grew up? What were they like at your age? Play cards or checkers. Bring your IPad and get on Luminosity and play that with them, it will help with their memory. If they don't say anything, just sit with them. They will feel important and perhaps your next visit they will engage. When time to leave, ask if it would be alright to give them a hug. The power of the human touch is healing. We all need to feel we matter. In doing this service, you will gain an insight on how to interact with people and you will become a more compassionate successful human being.

Tipping/Gratuity

Airport

Curbside check-in: $2.00 a bag.

Hotel

Doorman: He gets your car. Tip him $2.00 (tip when you are leaving only)

Bellman: He takes your bags to and from your room. Tip $2.00 a bag.

Housekeeping: $2–$5 daily. The reason daily is because there could be a different person from day to day. Use your discretion.

Uber/taxi/limo

A good tip would be 15% to 20%.

Bartender

A $1 per drink.

Server (Waitress/Waiter)

15% to 20%.

Usually if the party is 6 or more, the gratuity is already added to the bill.

In Europe, you don't have to tip as it is already included. But always make sure and then tip accordingly.

Salon Services

Aestheticians, manicurists, massage therapists, hair stylists, and barbers should be tipped 20%.

If there is a shampoo person, tip should be $3–$5.

If the owner of the salon works on you, it is customary not to tip.

Of course, use your own discretion.

Doctors

Of course, we do not tip them. However, I think it is a nice gesture to occasionally bring pastries, chocolates, a basket of muffins or fruit to the office in a show of appreciation.

Mailperson, Pool person, Gardener, Housekeeper

Or anyone else who does something for you on a regular basis should be given an end-of-year monetary gift. A bonus if you will for taking good care of your property. Use your discretion with each person and give from your heart with a nice note.

Kindness goes a long way!

Girls with Grace Lingo

Words and Adages and Actions in Which to Live

WE SAY:

Yes, instead of yeah.
No
Please
Thank you
My pleasure
I would love the opportunity to...

Avoid using "like" and "you know what I mean."

Instead of using "um" when at a loss for words, just breathe.

Use colorful adjectives along with: fine, great, good; venture out with others such as: fabulous, magical, delightful, swell, marvelous, joyful, copasetic, and lovely. Now you find more on your own!

When a friend gets engaged, we say "Best wishes" to the woman and "Congratulations" to the man.

Know when to speak!

> *Better to remain silent and be thought a fool than to speak and to remove all doubt.*
> —Abraham Lincoln

If you don't have anything nice to say, then don't say anything.

Don't judge a book by its cover.

When you point your finger at someone, you have three pointing back at you.

It is unacceptable for girls to hit one another!

It is unacceptable to swear in public. We must do our best to show our best at all times in public.

Keep ugly thoughts to ourselves.

When one needs to vent, do so with someone you absolutely trust and in private.

No name-calling; it is a sign of weakness.

If someone calls you a name or yells mean things at you, just smile!

No more "stinking thinking."

We are classy not trashy.

We don't chew gum in public.

Don't throw stones at glass houses.

We speak kind words to ourselves and others.

Yes, we all have "rights," but with "rights" come responsibilities!

Don't engage when someone is poking at you. Just smile and say, "Interesting." My Papa would always say, "Give someone enough rope to hang themselves." Meaning if you don't engage, it puts it back on them to examine their behavior.

Some helpful things I learned from Mel Robbins, the author of the book, *The 5 Second Rule.*

1. When running late for a meeting you are going to give a presentation: instead of running in and apologizing for being a bit late, say, "Thank you for your patience."

2. If someone bumps into you, don't say I'm sorry. Instead say, "Are you okay?" When we do this we are truly saying what we mean and we are empowering ourselves. We own our self-worth.

Add on to these and pass it on.

How to be a Good Roommate

WHEN CHOOSING A ROOMMATE, KNOW what you will tolerate and what you won't. Remember that you do not necessarily have to be friends. However, it is important that you get along and respect each other.

<u>Helpful Tips for Being a Good Roommate</u>

If you have the person you know you want to room with and you go together to find the right apartment, then everything should be split evenly (rent, deposit, cable, internet, gas, electric).

If you are renting a room out, then I think it is best to decide the total you want for the rent by including not only a portion of the rent (and you get to decide that); but also half of the electric, gas, cable, and internet. You need to charge a deposit fee (which will be given back the day the person leaves as long as there are no damages). and a cleaning fee. So it will be one lump total to be given to you the day before your rent is due. Make sure you draw up a rental agreement that you both sign. It is for both of your interest. It is not personal; it is business and this can save a friendship. This lays out what is expected and agreed upon.

I think it is best to get a maid service and then split that cost. Trust me, it will make your life easier and no one will feel they are taken advantage of.

Common Courtesies for Being a Good Roommate

Keep common areas clutter-free.

Don't have to always be asked to take the garbage out. When you see it is full, take it out. It doesn't take that much time. No excuses.

Clean up after using the kitchen. Wash dishes and put away. And if there is a glass or a few things of your roommate, it is a nice gesture to go ahead and wash theirs. Wipe down the counters and stove after using.

If you are sharing a bathroom be respectful and keep it clean.

Put the toilet seat and lid down.

Wipe the sink after using.

Pick up hair in the tub and shower.

Split the cost of toilet paper, paper towels, tissues, dishwashing soap and sponges.

Buy your own laundry products, hair, bath, teeth products.

If you borrow something, replace it. If it is something you find you are always using then when replacing it, buy one for yourself too! There is nothing worse than going to use something of your own and it is not there! Rule of thumb is if you use most of whatever it is, replace it and buy one for yourself.

Always ask before you use anything, and just because you were granted permission once, you still must ask every time you want to use or borrow something!

If you break something, admit it and offer to replace it.

Keep your TV and music at a reasonable level as to not keep the other person up or be distracting to them.

Learn to walk quietly. There are some people who I call "heel walk-ers." It is pounding. So be aware and make it a habit to walk softly. Girls, take off heels when coming in late.

If you are going to throw a party, ask your roommate if the date is okay with them. Always extend an invitation to them too; unless of course, it is a romantic dinner. Then have the party end at a reason-able time.

Talk with kindness when there is a need to clarify something that has been bothering you and then in fairness to the other person, ask if they have something they need you to know and work on. This is not a time to have hurt feelings, and then do a tit for tat.

Pick and choose your battles. Ask yourself, "In the scheme of things, is this worth fighting over?" Don't sweat the small things.

Remember the art of compromise.

Remember to treat people the way you would want to be treated.

Lastly, remember when living in an apartment you may have people above, below, and on either side of you, so be aware that manners matter. Many of the above examples also apply to your neighbors, such as walking and talking too loudly or playing your music/TV too loudly. When throwing a party remember to end at a reasonable hour. Never vacuum before 9a.m. and after 9p.m.

When we respect and value ourselves and others, life is more of a joy.

Managing
Your
Money

BANK

MANAGING YOUR MONEY

You're never too young to start understanding and managing money!

We should encourage our children to understand the value of money. Teach children that money comes from work. Give chores to your children and then pay them for some of the chores they do. Remember to make the work age-appropriate. It is only when we work that we make money. We then have money to buy the things we want. And when we work for what we want it feels good, like an accomplishment, not an entitlement.

It's okay to make mistakes with our money. When we are allowed at a young age to make mistakes with our purchases, we will learn the lesson then and save ourselves from making bigger mistakes when we are older. What we learn is once our money is gone, it is gone. So buy responsibly and within our means.

Make saving money a habit. If you don't save money, you won't have money. Saving money is the first thing you do. If we don't learn to save, we will go into debt for the things we want or need. And then when we are older, it will be difficult to get out of this because our money will be going to our debt instead of saving for our future.

Things we can to do to get us in the habit of saving are to open a savings account and a checking account.

Learn how to balance your checking account even though the bank now does this via your debit card. Keep a money journal. Have a column for outgoing money (debt), a column for deposits (credit) and then a column for the total (running balance).

The 50-30-20 Plan is as follows and is helpful in saving:

Your fixed and committed income expenses should make up 50% of your after-tax income. (Rent, car payment, insurance, bills)

30% is discretionary spending (Luxuries, vacation, clothes, etc.).

20% goes into savings.

But remember to put the 20% into savings first! If you need to cut your discretionary spending then, so be it.

Some Ideas for Saving Money

An easy way to start saving is to have a portion of your paycheck automatically put into a 401k. If you do not have one, have your bank automatically draft a certain amount each month and invest in a mutual fund. Start with 10% and once you get use to saving, you may want to increase to 20%.

Another way to save is to pay yourself 15%, then pay your bills, and rest goes into savings or mutual fund.

Starting at the age of thirty, put $100 a month in an IRA or a good investment accruing a high percent and do not touch it; then by the time you are sixty-five, you could possibly have half million dollars or more saved!

How do you do this? Cut out the Starbucks every day, cut out going lunch or dinner a few times a month. It will be well worth it. I wish I had this piece of information when I was thirty.

Also, when you no longer have a car payment, continue to pay your-self the car payment. Put half the sum in your savings account and half in an IRA or mutual fund.

Credit Cards

When in college, you can get a credit card. They help to establish good credit.

Only get a credit line of $500 to $1000 so that it is an easier amount to be able to pay back and not too big to get into trouble. It is always best to buy with cash and if you do not have the cash then you wait until you do.

Credit cards should only be used in emergencies and to buy plane tickets, rent a car or, if need be, to buy something online or an emergency.

Get in the habit of paying off the entire balance every month.

When the credit card people want to up your credit limit, do not let them. They want you to not be able to pay them back. That is how they make their money. Remember, you are in charge of your money. You dictate if and how much you want to up your credit limit. But remember to keep it at an amount that you can easily pay off.

Tips to Keep You on Track

Track your monthly spending. There are Smart Apps that let you track your budget: **mint.com** is one of them.

Don't be discouraged if you didn't learn the habit of saving at a young age. You can learn to be disciplined and make it a habit at any age. It may be challenging, but when we put our mind whole heart-edly in it, we do it!

Set aside money for unexpected expenses.

Own your worth!

Money should be looked as a wonderful thing. It is fun to save and fun to have money to experience life pleasures.

Remember to give to those less fortunate as it will come back a hundredfold to you.

Claim with praise and gratitude your financial freedom!

Barbara Stanny's words of wisdom on how to achieve financial freedom:

1. Save more.

2. Spend less.

3. Invest wisely.

4. Give generously.

Do them in this order, and you will have success and happiness!

Suggested Reading:

Allyson Lewis, *The Seven Minute Difference*

Tony Robbins, *Money: Master the Game*

Sharpening your brain

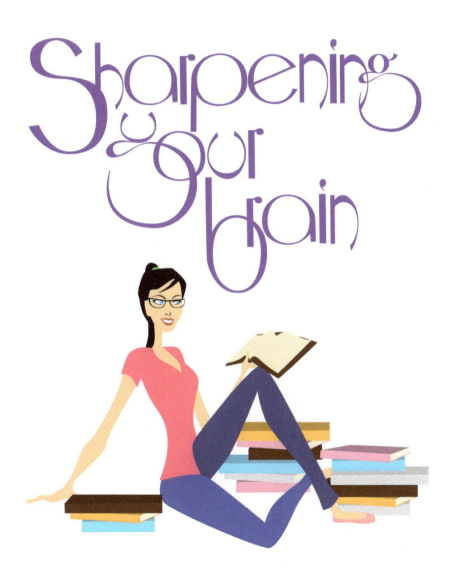

SHARPENING YOUR BRAINS

It is important to always have a thirst for knowledge. So how do we do this? ***Read!*** Get a library card. It doesn't cost money, and you have a plethora of books to choose from at your fingertips! Read the classics. Read about people you admire, history, the constitution, light-hearted books, feel good books, self-help books. Read newspapers. One that slants towards conservatism and one that slants liberal. That way you get both sides and can make an informed opinion for yourself.

Develop a good vocabulary. When reading, if you come across a word you don't know, then look it up. Put it on a note card and place it on your desk or mirror so you see it. Use it in a sentence at least three different times; this is how you will grow your vocabulary. Words are powerful, so think before using them and use the correct meaning as to not twist their meaning to push what you may want in life to manipulate others.

Talk to people!! Engage with people of different walks. Old people, coaches, people who do and have interests in what you do. Listen to their stories. Ask how they got where they are in life. People have fascinating life stories. We can learn much from sharing our thoughts and interests with one another.

Travel. Go to different states and countries. See how people live, learn about their culture. Enjoy the foods they eat. See the different sites that are indicative of that place. Open yourself up to a new adventure which will add to your life.

Join Groups

Church groups
Theatre group
Cooking classes
Book clubs

Engage in sports—tennis, golf, ski, walking, hiking, volleyball, swimming, horseback riding, and soccer, to name a few.

Political clubs—be open to learn and able to debate. Do not let yourself be indoctrinated or brainwashed, or to be politically correct or to lead with emotions. Emotions can be powerful, but they are not facts and are, therefore, misleading and can hurt rather than help in solving political challenges. Ask questions, do your own research, ask both sides. Look for the truth and the facts. Everyone has opinions, but opinions are not always the truth and are not all the time rooted in facts. Also, many say truth is relative, meaning your truth is yours but may not be mine. But there are absolute truths, the sky is blue, the grass is green, we need oxygen to breathe, and gravity, to name a few. One can say or slant it the way they want to achieve what they want, however, they are deceiving only themselves.

My Favorite Books and Authors

The following are just a few:

The Bible (greatest story ever told!)
Dr. Seuss, *Oh the Places You Go*
Ayn Rand, *The Fountain Head, Atlas Shrugged*
Leo Buscaglia, *Love, Personhood,* etc.
Marianne Williamson, *A Return to Love, Enchanted Love,* etc.
Bill and Ester Hicks, *Ask and It Is Given*

Rhonda Byrne, *The Secret, The Secret for Teenagers*
Stephen Covey, *Seven Habits of Highly Successful People*
Allyson Lewis, *The Seven-Minute Difference*
Malcom Gladwell, *The Tipping Point, Blink, Outliers,* etc.
Dan Millman, *Way of the Peaceful Warrior*
Don Miguel Ruiz, *The Four Agreements*
Chogyam Trungpa, *Shambhala: The Secret Path of the Warrior*
Sarah Ban Breathnach, *Simple Abundance*
James Galloway, *The Inner Game of Tennis*
Mel Robbins, *The 5 Second Rule*

Read philosophers such as, Thomas Aquinas, GK Chesterton, Aristotle.

Read self-help books; they inspire and empower.

Read autobiographies: people you admire and want to know more about their lives.

So many authors and so many books! Ask your English teacher for suggested readings of the classics.

Start a book club so that you can gather and then share your thoughts on what you read. This helps sharpen our social skills, as well as allows us to hone our abilities to formulate opinions.

Hillsdale College has online courses that teach on the Constitution, as well as many history and civics courses, all based on facts.

Prager University is another online site that has fascinating, factual, five-minute videos on many topics which give insights to history and culture and enable you to be informed and knowledgeable. I highly recommend both sites.

Read anything by Thomas Sowell. He is currently Senior Fellow at the Hoover Institution, Stanford University. He is well-informed and insightful as well as thought-provoking.

Again, get a library card and go to the library!

Personally, I love to hold a book, to be able to feel the pages as I turn them and the smell of books! Books that I feel I will read over, I then get in hardback to start a personal library.

A Kindle, an iPad and a Nook are wonderful to have as it enables us to have a library stored for travel.

Books take us places we have never been before. Meeting interesting people, going on adventures all without leaving from where it is we are reading.

Do Crossword puzzles, Sudoku puzzles, and games such as Luminosity on your computer and iPad. These keep our brains alert and sharpen our memories.

Another way to sharpen our brains and be well-rounded individuals is to engage in the Arts. You do this by going to the Ballet, the Opera, the Symphony, the Master Chorale, a Jazz concert, to Plays and to Museums. When you are there, engage not only your mind by learning who the artists, composers, choreographer, dancers, musicians are, but also engage your heart. What emotions do they evoke? Then share your thoughts with others because this is how we sharpen our social skills and become fascinating people.

<u>TV/Movies That Empower and Inspire</u>

The following are some of my favorites:

It's a Wonderful Life
The Bishop's Wife
Miracle on 34th Street
White Christmas
Holiday Inn
It Happened on 5th Ave
August Rush
Breakfast at Tiffany's

Bette Davis Movies

All This and Heaven Too
A Stolen Life
Now Voyager
The Letter
The Old Maid

Hepburn and Tracy Movies

Adam's Rib
Pat and Mike

The list goes on and on! As you can see I prefer the old movies. Actors such as: Charles Boyer, Spencer Tracy, Cicely Tyson, Sidney Poitier, Barbara Stanwyck, Glenn Ford, Katherine Hepburn, John Wayne, Audrey Hepburn, Cary Grant, Jimmy Stewart, Lana Turner, Hedy Lamarr, Rita Hayworth, Montgomery Clift, Marlon Brando, James Cagney and James Dean.

Then there are the brilliant English and Irish actors. Sir Laurence Olivier, Sir John Gielgud, Daniel Day-Lewis, Sean Connery, Gary Oldman, Jeremy Irons, Liam Neeson, Ben Kingsley, Pierce Brosnan, Eddie Redmayne, Maggie Smith, Helen Mirren, Kate Blanche, Judy Dench, Tilda Swinton, Vanessa and Lynn Redgrave are just a few.

Let me not forget musicals and the actors who brilliantly performed in them. Fred Astaire, Ginger Rogers, Gene Kelly, Rita Hayworth, Debbie Reynolds, Shirley MacLaine and the list goes on. Oh, let me not forget Doris Day, not only can she sing, but she is great at comedy, her movies are hysterical!

Another fun and enjoyable way to learn is to watch Documentaries.

The following are some TV shows I enjoy:

I love BBC/PBS Series: *Downton Abbey, Victoria, Father Brown, Call the Midwife*, to name a few.

<u>Netflix</u> has many great shows to enjoy. I love the Spanish shows, a few are: *Velvet, Cable Girls, Grand Hotel, A Time in Between,* and *El Internado.*

A few more of my favorites are: *13 Reasons, Alias Grace, The Paradise, The Killing, The Letters, Ripper Street, Lavender, To the Bone, Hidden Houses, Winter Sun, Girlfriends' Guide to Divorce, The Roosevelts: An Intimate History,* and so many more.

<u>Hallmark Channel</u> I love *When Calls the Heart, Ties that Bind.*

<u>Amazon Prime</u> has great shows and movies there such as *The Marvelous Mrs. Maisel.*

My passion is acting which is why this section has a long list of people and movies that inspire me. When I study these artists, I hone my craft which makes me a better actor. My point is: watch TV/Movies that you are interested in and actors you like.

You don't need to have cable to watch. Get a Roku or Apple Stick and watch what you want at a price you want.

Have a movie night with food and refreshments!

After watching a film, talk about them, share your thoughts. These are fun ways to make us more interesting. This is another way to add color to our personality. Be inspired!

DATING

DATING IS A RITUAL PASSED down through generations. Be the girl, and let the guy be the guy! Innately, we don't have to even think how to be. It is in our makeup. Courting is getting to know one another. Take it slow. Enjoy the journey. It is fun to discover the gifts a person has to offer.

Dating Tips

Let the guy call you. Of course, you can return his call, but let him make the first move! When you have been dating for a while, it is okay for you to initiate a call. Keep it short and never call when feeling insecure or needy.

Let the guy ask you out. Show that you are interested by a smile or hello. Don't play hard to get. It is difficult as it is for a guy to muster the courage to come talk to you.

Be true to yourself.

Dress for the date. Always neat and clean and smelling nice. Not too much makeup or perfume! Classy not trashy!

Let the guy open doors, bring flowers, walk on the traffic side, open the car door, stand up when you leave or enter a room. He is showing respect and manners. That he was brought up nicely. He is not saying you cannot do things yourself. Rather he is letting you know you are worthy of being treated correctly!

A gentleman always pays for the date. However, that does not mean a young lady should take advantage. A rule of thumb: Ask the guy what he is having and then order something you like in that same price range. This is you showing kindness and manners.

The more you date the same person, you can offer to take them out once in a while or treat for dessert or, when old enough, treat for the cocktails and appetizers. More than likely a gentleman won't let you, but will appreciate your kind gesture!

You can always have them over for lunch or dinner. You can bake them something. The adage is "the way to a man's heart is through his stomach." Remember, it is the act of doing something that shows you appreciate them.

When a time for a date is set and you find you are running late, then call to let the person know you are running late. Be honest with how long it will be until you are there. If the gentleman does not call to let you know he is running late, wait twenty minutes and then go do what you want to do. You then need to let the guy know (in a pleasant tone of voice, not an angry one) that it is unacceptable for him not to call to let you know that he has to cancel or that he will be late, and that you will not wait for him if he does not call. Of course, unless there was an accident! And the same goes for the girl. It is a common courtesy!

We must speak what is important to us so that the other person knows what is expected. Again within reason!

Find interesting things to do that you both enjoy. You do not have to love everything the other person does. You are two individuals coming together to share with each other and to bring the best out in one another.

Be yourself! If someone doesn't like you for who you are, then it is not meant to be. Move on!

Keep time for yourself and your friends.

Don't be needy; it is a sign of insecurity.

Bring out the best in each other.

Dating should be fun! If it is too hard, then more than likely, it is not the right fit. Move on!

Usually we know right away if we want a second date, so be honest! Say you enjoyed the date, but you don't feel a connection that goes beyond friendship!

Breakups are difficult and sad for everyone. Have the respect and integrity to talk to the person in person. Come from truth and kindness and love.

Every person who comes into our lives brings a gift and a lesson. So every experience is good as long as we can grow from it. It strengthens our beliefs in what we want and who we are. Most importantly, know you are worthy, always!

Do not do anything you do not want to. Only do things when you feel good about yourself, no matter the outcome. If someone puts peer pressure on you to act or do something against your belief, get away from them. That is not love! We must treat ourselves first with respect and dignity so that we can treat others the same.

Love never forces. Love inspires and empowers. Love helps us to shed what no longer is in our best interest. Love nurtures. Through our growth, love kindly brings good things forth.

On Marriage

15 Questions the Person You Marry Should be Able to Answer

1. Why do I love you?

2. Why do I want to spend the rest of my life with you?

3. Will I do my best to keep the romance alive? And How?

4. Will I grow with you and not away from you?

5. Will I stick through the rough times?

6. Am I willing to lose some battles to keep the peace?

7. Can I promise to put us ahead of everything else?

8. Will I be a great parent?

9. Will I be sure to remind you how much I love you regularly?

10. Can I promise to do all I can to keep that spark alive?

11. Will I support you even if you can't support you?

12. Will I promise to continue to pursue personal goals?

13. Will I not allow myself to let go?

14. If you are the first to go, will I be there with you until the end?

15. Can you promise me that if my time here is cut short, you will continue to live on for the both of us?

So there it is. I think it is great that we ask and answer so many questions. Throughout your time together, always be open to answer and ask important questions for it will keep you moving closer and forward. However, there needs to be a time where you walk the walk. When you both jump in the relationship and live it not just on paper. There are no guarantees in life, but if there is enough in common, then you need to go for it. God will guide you. But to just hold back until you know all the answers—well, that is never going to happen. You need to walk together living it, asking and answering the questions as you go. Actions bring results. You can be what one wants to hear on paper, but until you live it you will never really know. Actions speak louder than words.

Do not be that person who is always helping others understand love and teaching them how to love. They then become confident and are grateful, but then move on and marry someone else. Remember, you are not their mother or their therapist. Rather, be two adults coming together to grow and move forward together. Have someone who sees you, even the parts that are challenging, and know that you are for them. They see you make their life better. They don't want to change you because they see that you are always on the quest to better yourself. Instead they encourage you. You both bring out the best in one another, lifting up not tearing down. You both can stand back and see that you may have differences but in the whole picture those differences are what strengthen you.

Suggested Reading

The Rules by Ellen Fein and Sherrie Schneider
Mars and Venus On A Date by John Gray
He's Just Not That Into You by Greg Behrendt & Liz Tuccillo

WE NEED TO TEACH OUR **DAUGHTERS** THE DIFFERENCE BETWEEN A MAN WHO *FLATTERS* HER AND A MAN WHO *COMPLIMENTS* HER, A MAN WHO *SPENDS MONEY* ON HER AND A MAN WHO *INVESTS* IN HER, A MAN WHO VIEWS HER AS *PROPERTY* AND A MAN WHO VIEWS HER *PROPERLY*, A MAN WHO *LUSTS* AFTER HER AND A MAN WHO *LOVES* HER, A MAN WHO BELIEVES *HE IS GOD'S GIFT* TO WOMEN AND A MAN WHO REMEMBERS A *WOMAN WAS GOD'S GIFT TO MAN* AND THEN TEACH *OUR SONS* TO BE THAT KIND OF MAN

—Anonymous

goals

GOALS

Be/Do/Have

First BE the energy you call joy, love, wise, grateful, compassionate, etc.,

Then DO from that energy and this movement brings you to

HAVING what you want.

What you choose for yourself, give to another! Shine your light!

We create our life—good, bad, or indifferent! Therefore, we can change it.

When we discover something no longer serves us in a healthy way, release that behavior. We have grown and have reached our next level of enlightenment.

Something I have been contemplating on…

What if every day we woke up grateful knowing that God wants our best, has our best at hand, and created us at our best? Then if every day we just come with the thought that we are a work in progress and in that moment we are perfect, as we are, where we are right now and went on about our day with that thought. How would we react to everyone and everything we had to do that day? What more could we learn that would bring us to our highest self where peace would reside in us?

Albert Einstein once said, "A new type of thinking is essential if mankind is to survive and move to higher levels." When we try to fix something, sometimes we get stuck on what it is we want to change that we spend all our energies focusing on the challenge instead of the solution. Let us stop beating our heads against the wall time after time in the why-are-we-not-where-we-want-to-be in our lives. Why not look with new eyes at the challenge? Instead of wishing things were different, what if we saw those challenges not as a hindrance but a gift that leads us to our perfect next step on our path? I believe this is a breakthrough. It reminds us to be present, to feel the feeling and walk through it with courage. Knowing we are right where we are meant to be and going forward to where God wants us to be. To breathe in this new thought, knowing we are on our adventure walk of life that is divinely guided for our highest good. And in forging forward, we give gratitude for every person, place, opportunity we meet along our way which illuminates the path for enlightenment of our souls. We find compassion, forgiveness, healing, love, and renewal as we soar towards heaven.

Life is discovering, or should I say rediscovering, who we were created to be. Choices have consequences! When what we choose starts to feel uncomfortable, that is the nudge that alerts us to choose again! Every choice is ours, and every choice brings us closer to the beauty of our true self. So live joyfully on the journey! Know and believe that God is always with us, always loving us and always guides us to know when to choose again!

You will know who you were born to be when you experience peace, bliss! It may not be easy but it will not feel like work. You will be passionate about your life and all things will be added onto you! Above all, be kind and patient with yourself. St. Francis de Sale said it beautifully in this: "Have patience with all things, but first with yourself. Never confuse your mistakes with your value as a human being. You are a perfectly valuable, creative, worthwhile person simply because you exist. And no amount of triumphs or tribulations can ever change that." Wow! Let that wash over you, sit silently and ponder that powerful message. How does it make you feel?

And remember, no one can control us unless we give our power to them!

Goal Setting

In the book *Seven Habits of Highly Successful People*, which I highly recommend, Steven Covey gives many wonderful tools to assist you in succeeding. My two favorites were: utilizing the calendar and making a list.

Calendar

Get a calendar for the month and write what meetings and events you have on those dates. Be it class, a party, a meeting, and even the gym. Also, put the time you must be there.

This keeps you to a schedule, and then when someone asks you to do something, you can check your calendar. You will be able to answer either you can or you are sorry you have a previous commitment. You never have to tell someone what your commitment is. Some people may push you and say, "Come on, can't you change it," or "What do you have to do?" The best way to answer is to reiterate, "I am sorry, but I have a previous commitment." You can offer a different time or day.

If the person is so rude to badger you then you can reply by saying, "Again, I have a previous commitment and it is no longer open for discussion."

The reason for not telling them what the meeting is that if they ask you to meet for coffee, but it happens to be the time you go to yoga class they may say, "Can't you go to another class?" If we are pushed we sometimes acquiesce. Herein lies the problem. You got off your schedule and the thing that makes you feel better. You may not be able to fit it in later and then this might make you angry. In the long run, no one wants to be around us if we are unhappy. It is not selfish to take care of yourself. If you are happy, others around you will be happy. Be a blessing to yourself first so you can be a better blessing to others.

The calendar allows you to set your short term goals and accomplish them.

Goals/Lists

A LIST IS A TOOL to help you accomplish what it is you need to get done and keep you on track. It is a wonderful feeling when you cross things off your list. It makes you feel productive!

On a piece of paper or in a small book, write down everything you need to accomplish the next day. Organize it in the manner of importance, of time and getting from one place to the next efficiently. If there is something on the list you are dreading to do, put that first. That way you get it done and out of the way. Sometimes the thing we dread weighs on us, and if we don't get it done first, it consumes us the entire day and maybe into the next day. This is a waste of our energy!! More than likely, when we do it first we realize it wasn't that big of a deal, and we let out of sigh of relief.

Whatever we did not accomplish that day, move to the list for the next day.

The best time to make our list is at the end of each day. Trust me you will feel great when you are crossing of your list!

Whatever the mind can conceive and believe, it can achieve. (Napoleon Hill, from his book, *Think and Grow Rich*)

Goal Planning

MY BROTHER TOM TOLD ME once that "success occurs when our talent meets opportunity!" So be diligent in honing your talent and be prepared!

Purpose and Importance of Setting Goals

Once we state what we want, the energy goes out there and comes back to us. If you state something you do not want to happen, I always say, "Cancel. Cancel." That way it stops it from going out to the Universe and coming back to you. Dream big as you serve no one from playing small.

1. Rule

    a. Be precise. What do you want and what is your belief about what you want. How much you believe corresponds to the energy you put into achieving your goal.
    b. Be accountable. How and what do you do to get there.
    c. Be on schedule. How long will it take to achieve. Set a time frame to accomplish your goal.
    d. Award yourself. Do something nice for yourself for accomplishing your goal.

2. Scope

    a. short term
    b. medium term
    c. long term
    d. action goals

3. Wheel of life

    a. physical
    b. financial
    c. spiritual
    d. intellectual
    e. family
    f. social

Five Points to Developing a Goal Plan

1. Have an exact and clear goal.

2. Have a plan for your goal and a deadline for achieving it.

3. Have a strong desire and passion for the things you want in life

4. Have a strong belief in your own ability

My papa would always say, "If you want something to happen, you have to make the time."

No excuses!

Your attitude needs to be positive, your desire passionate.

Surround yourself with successful people. Doers!

Let go of people who bring you down, suck the life out of you and are naysayers.

Believe in yourself. Have a mentor.

Go the distance! When you fail, learn from it and make adjustments. Keep moving forward.

Do your best every day. Knowing your best will be different day to day. And that is okay, just do your best!

Visualization Board

WHAT IS A VISUALIZATION BOARD? It is where you put your goals that are written or in your head on a poster board so that you see them every day and call them forth.

Get whatever size poster board you want and then cut out words or pictures of the things you want and design the board in your creative way. Make it fun and enjoyable.

I myself have divided my goals into four boards:
Career
Health/exercise
Spirituality
Marriage

I cut out words and pictures that display what I want and have in my life. I love each one and look at them every day!

Make sure you put your board where you can easily see it. Words and how we speak are powerful, and when we see them written or in pictures, we are making them more powerful!

Prayer to God

To get something you never had, you have to do something you never did. When God takes something from your grasp. He's not punishing you, but merely opening your hands to receive something better. Concentrate on this sentence. The will of God will never take you where the Grace of God will not protect you.

—Author unknown

Who among us doesn't have an addiction of some sort? It's amazing what we will do to fill the void in our lives. We flee from our deepest loves and desires. Our choices and subsequent behaviors are often the complete antithesis to what our souls cry out for. Fear and convenience become the driving forces that propel us yet further from nourishing productive behaviors. The liberating element that I've observed in others serenity and have come to recognize in my own fleeting moments of sanity, can be encapsulate in one word…permission. Permission to risk, to fail, to succeed. Permission to live our lives to the fullest each day and respond to those passions we feel in the deepest parts of our souls.

—Author unknown

Bill Gates recently gave a speech at a high school about eleven things they did not and will not learn in school. He talks about how feel-good, politically correct teachings created a generation of kids with no concept of reality and how this concept set them up for failure in the real world.

Rule 1: Life is not fair—get used to it!

Rule 2: The world doesn't care about your self-esteem. The world will expect you to accomplish something *before* you feel good about yourself.

Rule 3: You will *not* make $60,000 a year right out of high school. You won't be a vice-president with a car phone until you earn both.

Rule 4: If you think your teacher is tough, wait till you get a boss.

Rule 5: Flipping burgers is not beneath your dignity. Your grandparents had a different word for burger flipping: they called it opportunity.

Rule 6: If you mess up, it's not your parents' fault, so don't whine about your mistakes, learn from them.

Rule 7: Before you were born, your parents weren't as boring as they are now. They got that way from paying your bills, cleaning your clothes and listening to you talk about how cool you thought you were. So before you save the rainforest from the parasites of your parent's generation, try delousing the closet in your own room.

Rule 8: Your school may have done away with winners and losers, but life *has not*. In some schools, they have abolished failing grades, and they'll give you as *many times* as you want to get the right answer. This doesn't bear the slightest resemblance to *anything* in real life.

Rule 9: Life is not divided into semesters. You don't get summers off, and very few employers are interested in helping you *find yourself*. Do that on your own time.

Rule 10: Television is *not* real life. In real life, people actually have to leave the coffee shop and go to jobs.

Rule 11: Be nice to nerds. Chances are you'll end up working for one.

A Fond Farewell

IN CONCLUSION, LET ME JUST say that I have learned much about myself writing this book. They say you teach best what you need to know the most.

I have always had a fascination with the 1940s and 1950s. I loved their style, how they had a zest for life, that they realized that family and friends are most important. So they made the time to spend with them. They took pride in their appearance regardless of their job or how much money they made. To look good is to feel good.

I want to empower us all to illuminate brightly! When we do this it is infectious and uplifting, not only to you but to others. You never know when the warmth of your light saved a soul!

I will leave you with one of my favorite quotes from Marianne Williamson.

> Our deepest fear is not that we are inade-
> quate. Our deepest fear is that we are powerful
> beyond measure. It is our light, not our dark-
> ness that most frightens us. We ask ourselves,
> Who am I to be brilliant, gorgeous, talented and
> fabulous? Actually, Who are you not to be? You
> are a child of God. Your playing small doesn't
> serve the world. There is nothing enlightened
> about shrinking so that other people won't feel
> insecure around you. We are born to make man-
> ifest the glory of God that is within us. It is not
> just in some of us, it is in everyone. And as we let

our own light shine, we unconsciously give other people permission to do the same. As we are liberated from our own fear, our presence automatically liberates others.

Be the light that shines so bright, be the light that only you can be. Just be the light that shines so bright, be the light that God created you to be. Go forth and Shine!

CPSIA information can be obtained
at www.ICGtesting.com
Printed in the USA
BVHW092303221019
561796BV00001B/1/P